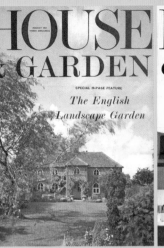
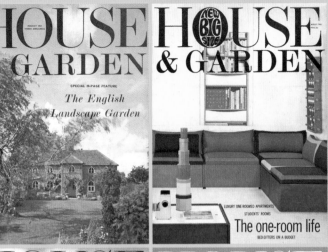

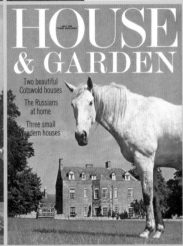
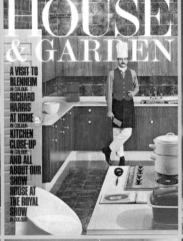

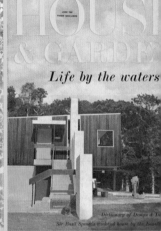
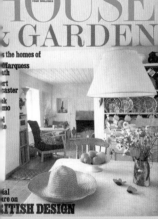
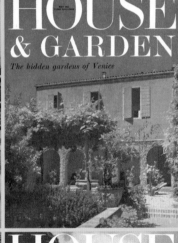

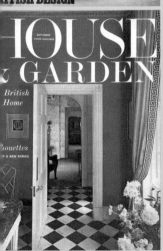
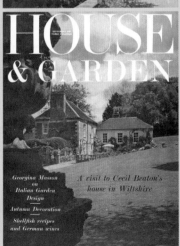
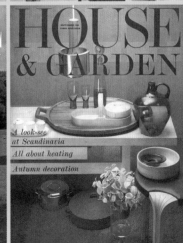
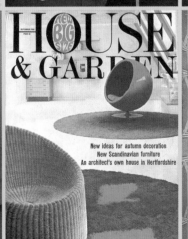

SIXTIES HOUSE

HOUSE & GARDEN

Catriona Gray
Foreword by Barbara Hulanicki

CONTENTS

FOREWORD

BY BARBARA HULANICKI

I grew up as part of a post-war generation when children were 'seen and not heard' – a period when Harrods would settle customers' bills once a year and where they sold copies of Georgian furniture in the Home Department. I could not wait to be free from the restrictions of so many rules and films became my visual influence for the home.

Times are very different now and it is difficult to convince young people today that at that time there was nothing good to buy in regular furniture or clothes stores. Instead, we hunted in junk shops and along Brick Lane at six on a Sunday morning when there would be a market for old (now antique), junk furniture. We would rush down to the East End to be the first to find treasures, things such as Pre-Raphaelite prints, Deco rugs and turn-of-the-century bookshelves. It was an adventure to hunt for what today are priceless pieces.

Things got exciting when the Lacquer Chest opened on Kensington Church Street, selling a stream of vintage goodies and bric-a-brac. I adored that store and couldn't stay out of it. On the other hand I avoided buying from modern design companies like G Plan and even today their furniture looks so formidable to me. When we needed kitchen furniture or kitchenware, we would traipse down to Habitat, which was full of amazing, modern ideas for dining and cooking; it had all the latest gadgets.

When the first Biba shop opened in a shabby side street off the even shabbier Kensington High Street, my husband Fitz and I hunted for Victorian hat stands to hang clothes off and used a French wardrobe as the centrepiece of the shop. It is difficult to imagine today how dark walls, very loud rock 'n' roll music and heavy drapes were deemed rebellious but parents would never enter our shop. Instead they would wait fearfully for their young ones outside the closed front door.

The girls' changing area was behind wobbly screens, which collapsed with the weight of the clothes piled up on them. Nobody, especially the boyfriends who waited on the purple velvet chaise longue, seemed to mind though. I found that particular chaise longue on the street one Sunday morning. There were no skips in those days and people would leave their old shabby furniture out on the street at the weekends for anyone to pick up.

I remember once discussing the latest luxury fad, wall-to-wall carpet, with George Harrison and Ringo Starr, at a party at Cilla Black's flat. Wallpaper also played a very strong part in the Sixties and Fitz and I commissioned Julie Hodgess to design large-scale Art Nouveau designs for the first two Biba shops. She printed the designs in gold and silver on heavy-duty wide photographic paper, which made it quite difficult to hang. Print was huge in the Sixties too and, after over-ordering on coat fabric, we produced countless leopard-print cushions at Biba.

This amazing book illustrates people's fearless use of patterns on patterns and countless other luxe Sixties trends. It's exciting to see how the interiors of the Sixties still look so up to date even today.

INTRODUCTION

'Rooms are for living in, and that is about the only collective statement that can be made about the design of today's interiors. If it is true that society is permissive, the same can be said of the design – or non-design – of the rooms we move around in. Anything goes.'

—SEPTEMBER 1968

From Pop art to Op art, plastic furniture to bubble-gum paint colours, the Sixties saw a new wave of interior design that was closely linked to popular culture and fashion. Design became increasingly youth-oriented, incorporating a playful, throwaway element that was designed to appeal to the new generation of baby-boomers. The UK in the Sixties underwent a cultural revolution, and the music, fashion and attitude of Swinging London became famous across the globe.

As air travel became more popular, the UK widened its international outlook. *House & Garden*, where the images in this book all come from, increasingly looked abroad for inspiration, and commissioned extensive colour features on design-conscious countries such as Sweden, France and the United States. Morocco also had an influence, as it became a popular destination on the hippy trail. Towards the end of the decade, interior design became progressively bolder and more psychedelic in colour.

International trends such as Pop art were translated into interior settings, and interior fashions became more accessible and affordable. The founding of Habitat by Terence Conran in 1964 created a new benchmark for how furniture was sold,

with showrooms where customers could see items styled in room sets, rather than having to pick items from catalogues. The rising generation of baby-boomers provided a willing market for products that had fun, light-hearted appeal, such as lava lamps and blow-up bubble chairs made out of brightly coloured PVC. In the same way that Pop art embraced consumer culture, design also harnessed the same sense of immediacy, celebrating the new and, at times, the throwaway – as seen, for instance, in the flat-packed cardboard chairs designed by Peter Murdoch that had an estimated lifespan of just a couple of months.

It is impossible to overplay the close relationship between popular culture and design during the Sixties, as artists and designers moved between genres. Peter Blake's art was visible in everything from the cover for The Beatles' album *Sgt. Pepper's Lonely Hearts Club Band* (1967) to advertisements for the Wool Marketing Board. Barbara Hulanicki opened Biba, whose Art Nouveau-inspired interiors popularized the trend for dreamy revivalism, helped along by the psychedelic movement. Interior designer David Hicks rose to prominence during this decade, with his bold use of pattern and ability to create

Right above
Plastic finds its way into virtually every component of this 1968 room.

Far right above
An Alexander Calder mobile tops off an impressive collection of modern art in the Milan flat of the Italian photographer Ugo Mulas in 1967. A Le Corbusier reclining chair is just visible in the foreground.

Right below
David Hockney made a variety of plywood trees to enliven his minimally furnished Notting Hill studio flat, pictured in 1969.

Far right below
A newbuild Paris apartment from 1964 mixes old with new. The adjustable metal-strip shelving and white walls contrast with the owner's collection of antiques.

schemes that were daring yet classically pleasing. David Mlinaric also created modern, elegant schemes, exemplified by his flat in Tite Street, Chelsea. Another leading decorator, Michael Inchbald, had a house on the same street as Mlinaric, and this was where his wife Jacqueline founded the Inchbald School of Design in 1960, signalling the rise of interior design as a recognized industry.

As interior design became more celebrated as a profession, *House & Garden* went through a period of exciting new collaborations across a variety of different media. It made a film on interior design for the flooring company Armstrong Cork, for which Olive Sullivan, the decoration editor, built three modern room sets in the photography studios at Vogue House. She was subsequently asked by the BBC to design a home for a young married couple. These collaborations, documented in within the pages of the magazine, show an awareness of the need to appeal to a younger, television-owning demographic.

House & Garden also designed schemes for Heal's and Harrods, as well as decorating show homes, and its substantial features show how adept the magazine was at curating new trends in interior design and capturing the zeitgeist of the Sixties. There was also an emphasis on showcasing new technology, such as developments in sound systems, which was extensively covered in a series of articles. Illustrated features provided an aesthetic alternative to using press images of furniture, and various illustrators were commissioned to produce black-and-white drawings for the magazine throughout the Sixties.

Above
Everything in this colourful 1964 sitting room is British. The curtain fabric – 'Phoenix', by Joyce Mattock for Tootal – complements the Alan Davie painting. Both the sofa and the upholstered chair were designed by Robin Day for Hille.

Right
Mary Quant pictured in 1967 in her flat in Draycott Place in Chelsea. The dining room – 'a delayed wedding present' to Quant and her husband from the interior designer Jon Bannenberg – had a circular table and seating, a black ceiling and louvred shutters made from metallic PVC.

These features provided round-ups of new developments in product design and gave a very comprehensive overview of changing fashions in furniture. Some of these illustrations can be seen in the chapter on furniture in Part Three of this book.

This decade saw the magazine run substantial interviews with legendary designers from Madeleine Castaing to David Hicks, and *House & Garden* also chronicled developing trends as they happened, whether it was the latest developments in blow-up furniture or the phenomenal success of Habitat. Edward Bawden illustrated a feature on Dublin's architecture; David Gentleman produced a series of woodcut prints that were bound into copies of the magazine; and Cecil Beaton's sets for the film version of *My Fair Lady* (1964) were carefully photographed.

The magazine also chronicled the most stylish international interiors of the decade, and these are the focus of this book. Part One looks at the Sixties house, room by room. Part Two shows complete houses including an assortment of homes belonging to leading designers, artists and taste-makers, from Mary Quant to Barbara Hulanicki. Finally, Part Three looks at the decoration – the furniture and fabrics, glassware and ceramics – that is so essential for lending style and flair to any living space, no matter what the decade.

1. ROOMS

HEART OF THE HOUSE
THE KITCHEN

'Everyone now wants a kitchen which is a cross between a clinical laboratory and a cosy night-club. On the one hand, it should be a suitable place for culinary experiments to be carried out in relative solitude, on the other a place where friends can foregather, chatting up the hostess whilst she prepares their delicious meal.'

—JULY/AUGUST 1968

Left
The focus of this 1968 London kitchen is its T-shaped central island. Covered with stainless-steel tiles, it incorporates a hob, sink, chopping board and waste-disposal unit. A row of cork-covered cupboards provides discreet storage for food and culinary paraphernalia, while red freestanding beams contrast with the period cornicing.

Right
Toile de Jouy walls and a Provençal floor create the feel of a rustic farmhouse interior. It is all an illusion, however: both walls and floor of this 1968 kitchen are covered in patterned vinyl.

Two different aspects of a 1968 kitchen in Kensington, which was also used as the main entertaining area. The floor tiles were imported from Italy by the owner, and the collection of copper saucepans on the floating pine shelf were decorative as well as practical. Louvred doors enabled the cooking area to be screened off when necessary.

Below right
Toile de Jouy appeared time and again in style-conscious kitchens. This one made the cover of *House & Garden* in July/August 1967. The combination of traditional china, veneered units and varnished pine was very on trend in the Sixties.

Right
Formica work surfaces, a 'Transatlantic' cooker by WH Paul, and walls covered in brown lino create a sleek look. This picture was used to illustrate a feature written by the architect Richard Rogers in August 1963, which stressed the importance of designing kitchens that were functional rather than laden with appliances.

Left
This 1969 kitchen was built in a Gothic Revival country cottage dating from the early nineteenth century. The young owner was an architect and worked with the space, installing a breakfast bar that doubled as a food-preparation area, with additional storage space above it.

Below
This is a 1969 display kitchen from the Building Centre in London's Camden Passage with units by Christien Sell. The wicker basket was considered an essential decorative accessory – although it is doubtful if it had practical value in urban homes.

How to combine functionality with a sociable layout was the question that dominated kitchen design during the Sixties. Regardless of age, class or income bracket, homeowners wanted a kitchen that functioned as the heart of the house: a space for cooking, eating and entertaining.

This was a relatively new development. Before American-style kitchens had become popular in the Fifties, and before social changes following two world wars had made full-time cooks in private houses a thing of the past, the kitchen had been a rather neglected room, frequently located in the basement of a house, with antiquated, functional equipment and little, if any, thought given to its decoration.

With the advent of innovative electrical appliances such as fridge-freezers and washing machines, alongside sophisticated new cookers, the kitchen suddenly became the focus of newlyweds' attention. Cookery writers celebrated the use of new ingredients as well as the exploration of

Below
By 1960 cookers were the most sophisticated piece of kitchen equipment. At the back are two cookers that incorporate rotisseries – the one on the left is by Tappan; the one on the right is by Moffat. In front of these are a mix of gas and electric cookers by (from left) Tricity, Main, G.E.C., New World, Cannon and Allied Ironfounders.

Right
In 1963 Heal's teamed up with the Gas Board to create an exhibition to show how it was possible to have a kitchen and sitting area in the same room. This room set displays the kitchen part: beyond it, you can see a set of curtains, as kitchen segues into sitting room beyond the fitted units with their distinctive metal-fronted cupboards.

exotic cuisines, and this further fuelled the
desire to spend more time in the kitchen.

It is impossible to overstate the influence
that the United States had on modern
kitchen design. What is now standard –
the open-plan layout, island worktops and
fitted units – had its origins in the States.
While the Fifties kitchen had celebrated
technological advances with a modern,
clean-edged appearance – bright reds
and yellows, linoleum flooring, plastic
appliances, Formica surfaces – the Sixties
saw a change in the way that kitchens
were decorated. Although the style of the
preceding decade persisted for a time, the
Sixties saw the introduction of a softer,
country style that was more informal and
conducive to a relaxed approach to living
and entertaining.

When the first fridges and electric
cookers had appeared in kitchens before
the Second World War, they were seen as
very clinical, futuristic items. They came
in varying sizes and were often unwieldy;
little thought had been given as to how they
would integrate with the other appliances
and furniture. The American influence,

however, had standardized these appliances and introduced the idea of fitted units for a homogenous, unified feel. This look was the accepted face of kitchen design by 1960, but during the following decade the kitchen began to acquire an added level of character.

In the early Sixties, cool colours were popular, with sleek units and stainless steel finishes. As the decade progressed, a more relaxed look came into fashion. In urban, modern homes, colour reappeared, but in a less primary way than in earlier years – warm tones and patterns were popular, teak and beech were increasingly used as work surfaces, and splashbacks were often tiled with colourful abstract designs. This tied in with designs for ceramics, which often sported bright, abstract patterns, or stylized floral or Eastern motifs. In Britain, Hornsea Pottery – a relatively new company – was popular thanks to its innovative tableware that typically had matt white backgrounds with impressed linear or geometric designs, coloured in to create a modern effect. A similarly successful company was Portmeirion, which had a number of popular patterns – 'Totem', 'Variations' and

'Magic City', among them – that found their way onto many a style enthusiast's dresser.

The country look also became very popular, and this manifested itself in the reintroduction of rustic furniture, most commonly in pine. Copper pans came back into fashion, as they created a traditional atmosphere, as did Delft-style blue-and-white or red-and-white tiles. As the kitchen moved centre stage, it was its functional yet warm farmhouse avatar – be it British or French – that provided an alternative model to its urban American counterpart. In the Sixties, new products began to reflect the country look. Chairs with woven-rush seats surrounded simple kitchen tables in pine

or oak, while wicker baskets were a popular accessory for those seeking to add a rustic accent to their kitchen. Painted wooden furniture was also common, although it faced strong competition from unpainted pine in terms of popularity. The inclusion of antique pieces of furniture also added to the country-kitchen atmosphere.

Sometimes urban and rustic styles were even used in conjunction with each other, creating a bewildering juxtaposition of influences in which clinical, modernist surfaces of stainless steel might be found beneath a Provençal-inspired splashback of terracotta tiles. This influx of new options for kitchen design both raised the

bar for home-owners seeking to create new and interesting schemes, and created innumerable potential pitfalls for the amateur decorator.

Alongside all this was a real enthusiasm for the ways in which domestic appliances were evolving. With space travel becoming a reality and rapid advances in other areas of technology fuelling public awareness of scientific possibilities, an interest in gadgetry led people to consider the potential developments of the items that serviced their home.

Appliances that we now think of as standard – dishwashers, for example – were still fresh on the market in the Sixties, and

Left
Egg-yolk yellow kitchen units and a cork floor create a sunny feel in this spacious 1968 kitchen. Note the use of natural materials that add to the warm colour palette: the untreated wood beams, the rattan sofa, the dining chairs and the strip of wood beneath the Formica worktops.

Below left
A wood-lined ceiling and expansive windows make for a modern kitchen. Shown in 1963, this Yorkshire house is furnished simply, with great emphasis placed on functionality.

Bottom left
This 1965 kitchen is on the ground floor of a Victorian conversion. Designed by Michael Inchbald, it has pine-clad walls and the ceiling is covered in a floral paper from Cole & Son (then known as Cole's).

Below right
Here a kitchen has been installed in a rather narrow space. This photograph is from 1968, but the interior has a timeless quality, thanks to the white tiles that cover the walls, the monochrome units and an assortment of ceramics from different periods.

Left
This country kitchen was originally designed in the early Fifties, but was given a 1967 update that introduced a new cooker and dishwasher, as well as some more modern kitchen units. The overall effect was extremely practical and well planned.

Below left
Chequered floor tiles, a specially installed porthole window and an eclectic mix of furniture create atmosphere in photographer David Bailey's Sixties kitchen in Primrose Hill, London, pictured in 1969.

Below right
A striking tiled floor by Casa Pupo creates an attention-grabbing 1967 kitchen. The effect is heightened by the cobalt-blue walls, curtains in Lucienne Day's 'Apex' print and the inexpensive reproduction advertising poster on the back of the kitchen unit.

Following pages
Wood veneer and a geometric-patterned wallcovering make for a style-conscious, late-Sixties kitchen. The lino is equally striking and runs from the scullery to the dining and cooking area.

as a result there was a considerable amount of debate and experimentation concerning their function. 'Why, after all, shouldn't washing machines wash dishes as well? Why not utilize oven heat trapped in the hood of a cooker and conduct it out as clean warm air?' asked *House & Garden* in a 1965 article on multi-purpose kitchen equipment. The accompanying illustrations show an ambitious variety of experimental kitchen equipment. Sadly, neither the ironing-board-cum-bar-table nor the kitchen unit that encompassed a mind-boggling union of sink, waste-disposal unit, washing machine, dishwasher, scourer, mixer *and* silver polisher has survived the test of time.

AN AESTHETIC FREE-FOR-ALL
THE SITTING ROOM

'No aesthetic movement of recent times had had so explosive an effect upon the eyes and minds of the lay public as pop art and none so immediate an effect upon the backgrounds of the younger generation. Of all art movements this is the one that deserves to be termed an applied *art, however negligible its merits as a* fine *art. Few art movements have thrown up motifs which were derived from – and can be matched in – the local supermarket and applied with equal gusto to the front of a sweater or the wall of a sitting room.'*

—AUGUST 1965

Left
An Eero Saarinen 'Tulip' chair is at the centre of this precise 1965 scheme, with other pieces by H K Furniture from Heal's. Heal's also imported Danish lighting – seen here are a pair of white hourglass table lights and a striking pendant shade. Even the plain white ashtray was imported from Finland.

Above
This room channels Italian style, *circa* 1965. The 'San Luca' chair and 'Arco' lamp are both by Achille and Pier Giacomo Castiglione. A tiled floor and marble tabletop continue the Italianate feel, as does the contemporary painting by Leonardo Cremonini.

Below

Two mirrored walls create a mind-bending effect in a 1967 sitting room. The spherical 'Bomb' chair is by Finnish designer Eero Aarnio, while the 'Catrena' dining chairs were by Brian Long for Heal's. Modular polystyrene box units are decorated with 'House of Cards' playing cards by Charles Eames.

Right

The curtains and tablecloth are two colourways of a Barbara Payze design for David Whitehead. The armchair is from Greaves and Thomas while the sofa is G-Plan. A hand-woven rug brightens the marble-tiled floor, while another shot of colour comes from the yellow enamel jug.

Below left
Strong colours dominate this sitting area from 1961. A dash of black and white is introduced by the Edward Bawden *Liverpool Street Station* linocut print and, below it, by Piero Fornasetti's 'Head' and 'Foot' plates.

Below right
In this 1969 scheme, the eye is drawn to the leather and aluminium chair, designed by Finnish designer Ilmari Lappalainen for the Swedish furniture company Asko. Behind it is a 'Little Boxes' storage unit by James Schaffer for Stone and a lamp by Kienzle.

Below left
In keeping with the Sixties idea of
mobility, a sitting area was set up in the
Ewan Phillips Gallery in Mayfair in 1968,
with lightweight chrome and canvas
furniture from Omk. The paintings are
by Halima Nalecz, while a Henry Moore
sculpture and Eva Springerova's *Kneeling
Woman* are also on show.

Below right
Curtains in 'Vanessa' by Hilary
Rosenthal for Bernard Wardle catch
the eye in a 1966 sitting room. The
By the River poster was designed by
John Burningham for London Transport.

With the emergence of Pop art came a new attitude to interior decoration. As may be deduced by the slightly acerbic tone of the quotation on page 33, it was never really accepted as a serious interior design trend, but was rather considered as a youthful, transitory style of decoration whose bright, consumer-oriented aesthetic mirrored the Sixties zeitgeist. It manifested itself in brightly coloured accessories and textiles, and in plastic furniture – whether in boldly coloured, tough polypropylene or in the new trend for PVC blow-up furniture.

Many of the decorative staples of Pop art were made from cheap, flimsy materials, with designers revelling in the transitory quality of their designs. Blow-up chairs could be deflated and packed away in a suitcase, while Peter Murdoch's colourful cardboard chairs were designed for maximum visual impact, but were never intended to be long-lasting. Posters became popular as an art form, and ranged from the much-coveted originals of artists such as Toulouse-Lautrec, Mucha and Steinlen, to cheap reproductions. While Andy Warhol was at the forefront of the Pop art movement in the United States, the UK was quick to embrace the style and adapt it to suit its own popular culture.

Below
Traditionally favoured for conservatories, rattan furniture became a popular choice throughout the house during the Sixties. Here it has been used to create a modern scheme in a living area that doubles as a study – although it has to be said that it slightly evokes the atmosphere of a waiting room.

Below right
The Scandinavian furniture in this 1961 room was all sourced from the Norwegian furniture company Westnofa. The black chipboard walls are enlivened by a Scandinavian wool rug.

As an interior design trend, it was not one for the purists. *House & Garden* noted: 'a movement offering such tremendous scope for the demonstration of the ego has appealed to those who regard their homes as ebullient foregrounds (some might say fairgrounds) for their lives, rather than as restful background.' Like the artistic genre itself, it was a break with tradition, and was an aesthetic free-for-all where all traditional preconceptions of design could be flouted. It signalled a celebration of the modern and of all the noise and brashness that went with it; it chronicled the world of the supermarket, garage, motorway and cinema. The main trick was to avoid half measures, and blend raw, anti-traditional forms of furniture with lots of bright colour. Floorboards, woodwork and walls were typically painted white to act as a counterfoil to the eye-popping accessories and artwork.

In 1965 *House & Garden* published photographs of the house of the wealthy New York insurance broker Leon Kraushar, who had turned his home into a shrine to Pop art with the aid of American decorator David Barrett. 'I love pop art,' Leon Kraushar says in the article, 'because it shows the life we live today. It's not the past, it's not history, it's *my* life, the life *I* am living. It's the American landscape, with its billboards, its highways, its hamburgers, its filling stations, its wonderful consumer goods. When I go to the supermarket, I see Brillo boxes just like the ones by Andy Warhol in my foyer, and when I come home, this makes my "Brillo Boxes" even more pleasurable.'

Britain's heyday for Pop was in the mid-Sixties, with flat stylized imagery and 'flower power' motifs embodying the spirit of Swinging London. This imagery was reflected in the homes and businesses of the new generation who were creating the music, fashions and art that were having an international influence. By the end of the decade, however, a different influence had come into play, characterized by a renewed interest in antiques and Victorian design.

In general, the widespread enthusiasm for the Scandinavian look persisted throughout the Sixties. But it was beginning to lose the cutting-edge cool it had enjoyed in the previous decade, when the UK, finally free from wartime restrictions on furniture, had belatedly embraced the modernist aesthetic that that had first become popular in mainland Europe in the Thirties. Still, Scandinavian style had become synonymous with mainstream good taste, and formed the backbone of the typical sitting room created by style-conscious owners who had not inherited or hunted out antique furniture.

Left
Wood abounds in this 1964 scheme, from
the pine coffee table to the ash sideboard
and the cane and beech armchair with
leather arms, designed by Martin Francis.
The curtains are 'Gillyflower' by Gillian
Farr for Conran Fabrics.

Below
Floor-to-ceiling glazed windows create
an airy sitting area in a modern house in
Surrey, pictured here in 1961. The eye is
drawn to the different coloured furniture,
which adds a playful element to the room.

Because of this, the sleek lines of so many
early to mid-Sixties interiors discouraged
clutter, and the favoured look for much
of the decade was simple, with large,
bold pieces of ceramics and glass. Teak
bowls with curved, sculptural forms were
popular, as were small abstract sculptures
in wood, metal or marble. Tastes became
more bohemian and eclectic as the decade
progressed, and a more relaxed look
appeared. The sitting room was the place to
display collections of curios and antiques
– massed displays of Staffordshire dogs or
figures, model ships or other memorabilia.
This taste for displaying collections
would become increasingly popular in
the Seventies, as styles became even more
eclectic and nostalgia for the past became
more pronounced.

As air travel became more commonplace
during the Sixties, the influence of other
cultures found its way into the sitting room.
Indian textiles and art were particularly
influential, and were a source of inspiration
to such designers as David Hicks. Stronger,
darker colours – oranges, purples and yellow
ochres – became more prevalent, and the
richly patterned wallpapers produced at
the top end of the market offered a more
sophisticated alternative to the cheap
poppy florals and psychedelic motifs aimed

Left
A 1966 room with a strong Scandinavian theme – the poster on the wall is a bit of a giveaway. At this time, the Knightsbridge department store Woollands imported a quantity of Swedish stock, a selection of which was used here.

Below
White ceramic floor tiles, white walls, paper birds and a painted fretwork ceiling, lit from above, create a striking living space in 1967. The chair and table in the background are by Finnish designer Ilmari Tapiovaara; the cube table in the foreground is by Albrizzi; the storage units are by Conran.

Below right
In the Sixties, Heal's imported Swedish rugs which found their way into many a stylish sitting room, as here in 1964. Above the Alvar Aalto dining table is a cube-shaped pendant light by the Finnish designer Svea Winkler.

at younger consumers. Despite all this emphasis on colour, monochrome was still in evidence too. Now, however, it had morphed from the clean-lined, modernist look of the Fifties towards the complex patterns of Op art, as epitomized by the young British artist Bridget Riley, whose home is pictured on pages 104–7. The sheer volume of new and different influences that were present in interior design during this decade resulted in an extraordinary variety of styles. Thanks to the carefree, transitory attitude that pervaded this area, the most attention-grabbing styles could be created even on the tightest of budgets.

Left
The 1967 view from the living room to the dining room of the house Richard Rogers designed for his parents in Cheam in the mid-Sixties. Walls are white and the floor beneath the famous Eames chair is pine parquet, while the dining room table is a huge slab of green marble.

Below
During the Sixties it became more acceptable to leave wood untreated. Here, in 1961, a pine partition and shelves – upon which stands another Sixties decorative staple, the cheese plant – make for a simple sitting room. The rough parquet floor adds to the rustic feel.

Below right
These striking Scandinavian ash, steel and black-leather chairs were imported by Liberty, while the marble-topped table in this 1961 sitting room was designed by Charles Eames. Just visible on the wall is *Spring Hat* by Sally Ducksbury.

A SENSE OF OCCASION
THE DINING ROOM

'Any discussion of the comparative merits and demerits of dining area versus dining room is apt to be heated by prejudice. People are inclined to argue too subjectively, defending what they've got. As in the rest of the domestic world, answers are made basically by necessity, but part of the pleasure of discussion is the chance it offers for stating one's own ideal setting, given no obstacles, financial or spatial.'

—NOVEMBER 1966

Left
A 1966 dining room with a strong Scandinavian influence: the tablecloth was imported by Danesco, while the tableware was from Upsala-Ekeby as were the red dining chairs with woven-cord seats. The walls are covered in a pine veneer, which was imported from Sweden.

Above
With a dining table by Arne Jacobsen, a Kai Kristensen dining chair and teak settee units by Aakjaer Jørgensen of Bramminge, this 1961 scheme celebrates Danish design. All the tableware, aside from the Holmegaard glasses, is by Jens H Quistgaard for Dansk Designs.

Below
In this image of a Holland Park house from 1969, orange is the dominant colour in the dining room. A Cole & Son wallpaper decorates the walls, with a pair of French art-nouveau posters and a set of Pop-art prints.

Right
A carpet designed by Jacqueline Groag and Eero Saarinen's 'Tulip' chairs and table combined with a light by the Italian designer Sergio Asti for Kartell, create a strikingly modern scheme in this 1968 dining room.

The myriad of decorative influences that were present during the Sixties emboldened attitudes to interior design. The dining room, as a place dedicated to sociability and conviviality yet less frequently used than the sitting room, was the ideal place to experiment. New trends could be given a trial run, with minimum daily impact if the results were less than desirable. It was also a good place to display treasured possessions, from paintings and statues to smaller collections of antiques or curios. However, a room devoted solely to the purpose of dining was becoming something of a rarity in post-war new-builds – architects were now favouring open-plan layouts that cut down on building costs and gave a greater sense of spaciousness within the same area, unimpeded by dividing walls. As a greater emphasis was placed on a multi-purpose living area, the dining room was becoming the preserve of older houses.

Below
From the Japanese paper lampshade to the 'Cesca' chairs by Marcel Breuer that surround the dining table, design staples abound in this room from 1966. The top-of-the-range radio was designed by Robin Day for Pye.

Bottom left
This 1963 photograph shows an assortment of objects arranged on the shelves of Terence Conran's home by his wife Caroline, who had previously worked as an assistant to *House & Garden*'s decoration editor Olive Sullivan.

Bottom right
An example of the trend for cheap, collapsible furniture: this 1967 plywood table could be dismantled and packed away in minutes.

As more people chose to eat in the kitchen or the sitting room, this created the need to create a dining area within these spaces. Keeping the dining area close to the food preparation area was the most logical solution, but in flats where kitchen space was restricted, a dining table and chairs could be set up in the sitting room instead. This space was often demarcated by a different type of flooring, or perhaps a hard-wearing rug if the floor was carpeted in the white shag-pile that became fashionable in the Sixties. Layouts that were truly open-plan worked best, as the kitchen, dining and sitting areas could all coexist harmoniously.

Modern furniture was designed to suit these layouts, and companies such as Ercol produced dining tables, chairs, armchairs, sofas and side tables all in the same style, enabling a sense of continuity to be created within the open-plan space. This look was very much associated with the Fifties, however, and, as the Sixties progressed, colourful plastic furniture began to replace the Scandinavian teak. Bolder, patterned wallpapers meanwhile created a more playful look than the serious approach of the previous decade, which had been more directly inspired by modernism.

Below
British design makes an appearance in this 1969 scheme, with white lacquered 'Form Five' units from G-Plan and an Axminster carpet. The chairs and lamp are by Walker, Wright, Schofield.

Right
Synthetic materials create a 1968 dining room with a difference. The table by Keith Welters has a Perspex base and a plate-glass top, while the accompanying Perspex chairs have vinyl seats. As you might have guessed, the floor is also covered in vinyl.

Whether it was a dining room or dining area, good lighting was essential to any well-designed scheme. A small dining room could be given an intimate atmosphere; a large, cavernous one could be imbued with warmth; while a dining area within an open-plan layout could be given distinction and autonomy through the correct use of lighting. At the start of the Sixties, the style of Fifties lighting design was still very much in evidence – seen in symmetrical forms, bright colours, hourglass shades and etiolated brass stems. These shapes were inspired by Italian design, but they faced stiff competition from the more restrained lights that were now being imported from Scandinavia, with the 'PH' ceiling lights of the well-established Danish designer Poul Henningsen especially promoted as examples of good lighting design. The 'PH' lights had symmetrical graduating louvres that diffused light evenly and prevented a harsh, overhead glow. Henningsen's ideas and designs were widely adopted during the Sixties, especially by other Scandinavian companies such as Lyfa and Fog & Mørup. The Danish influence can also be seen in the teak-and-brass table lamps and standard lamps that were produced by many British manufacturers.

Below left
The sunny colours of walls and curtains in this 1968 room set are emphasized by a Moroccan rug from Liberty and a table set with Cornish Gold Ware.

Below right
A triptych of framed prints is the crowning glory of this trippy 1969 dining area. With furniture and kitchen units all in white, the patterned purple wallpaper and green lino floor provide the colour.

Below
This all-white room from 1969 is part
conservatory, part dining room, and was
built as an extension to a living room.
The walls are covered in embossed tiles.
Stacking chairs designed by Joe Colombo
surround an Arkana table.

British designers also contributed to
Sixties lighting. Stag Furniture designers
John and Sylvia Reid were consultants
for lighting manufacturers Rotaflex and
produced the popular 'Mettalux' range;
Best & Lloyd produced some notable
modern designs; Peter Nelson's company
Architectural Lighting Ltd introduced a
range of minimalist aluminium table and
floor lamps in 1962, while Anglepoise lamps
remained as popular as ever.

Aluminium had become the most
common material for the ceiling and wall-
mounted spotlight systems that appeared
in the second half of the decade, providing
flexible and focused lighting. In contrast
to these simple, classic models, the latter
part of the Sixties saw the arrival of more
light-hearted designs with a novelty value in
keeping with the pop-culture influence that
was aimed at younger consumers. The lava
(or 'Astro') lamp was invented by the UK
designer Edward Craven Walker in 1963.
This contained a mixture of oil and coloured
wax inside a glass container – when this
mixture was heated by a light bulb, the
illuminated blob of wax would constantly
shift and alter in shape. Lampshades
printed with psychedelic motifs or 'flower
power' Pop-art patterns were also sold
widely, while Habitat produced colourful
enamelled pendant lights and flat-packed
shades that, when assembled, made eye-
catching geometric shapes.

By the late Sixties, plastic lighting became
much more commonplace. It increasingly
replaced Bakelite lamps, as these tended to
crack when they were hot or if they suffered
a knock. Plastic lamps and shades were
much tougher and could be produced in
a limitless number of shapes. Because of
this, clear or tinted plastic was often used to
replace glass. Many of the most innovative
designs came from Italy, such as Vico
Magistretti's organic-shaped 'Dalu' table
lamp and Joe Colombo's lamps for Kartell.

Still, stylish as these products were, the
average British homeowner was rather
reluctant to introduce plastic into their
dining rooms and in general it was left to a
younger generation to purchase the more
avant-garde designs. With stainless steel
cutlery increasingly replacing the old silver
services, and transfer-printed contemporary
designs on china echoing the colours and
motifs that were appearing on textiles and
wallpapers, the act of dining, even if it was
confined to a corner of the kitchen, could be
imbued with a sense of occasion.

A SIMPLER STYLE
THE BEDSIT & STUDIO ROOM

'Some people go in for lots of clutter in a small room, producing something like a nest, but I think this is a mistake. The minimum furniture and objects produce a much more interesting result. A small room can take something really large – a piece of furniture, a picture, or even an enormous piece of sculpture. It is bittiness and the tentative approach to design in the home that pays the meanest dividends.'

—JUNE 1963

Left
A bright screen-printed fabric – 'Aurora 3' by Genia Sapper for Moygashel – is used for walls and bedcover in this compact bedsit from 1969.

Above
Untreated wood paired with sheepskin rugs on floor and bench give this 1962 studio a Scandinavian feel. The substantial skylight makes the most of the natural light and adds to the airy atmosphere of this attic space.

Below left
The two 1965 pictures below show two different angles of the studio of British painter Brian Rice, whose abstract works can be seen on the walls. A striped sofa continues the vibrant theme, as does the striped throw that covers the bed.

Below right
A 1965 studio room designed for a young textile designer who worked and lived in the same space. To the left, the corner of a screen is just visible: this was to conceal a small stove used for cooking.

Right
Much of the furniture in this self-contained 1968 room is from Heal's. Although the design looks very urban, it was actually the self-contained guest room of a modern house in the Chilterns.

Left
The design of this studio and study from 1969 is cheap and cheerful, with modular, easy-to-assemble storage and a pair of fold-out wooden tables used as both work area and dining space, as well as the ubiquitous Japanese paper lantern.

Below left
Furniture from Heal's creates a practical workspace in a large 1961 room that also doubles as a living area. The painting is by John Bratby.

Below right
This 1966 room might be furnished with the bare essentials, but these are the best that money can buy. The desk chair is from Heal's and the rosewood cabinet is from Liberty. On the wall are prints by Edward Bawden. The sofa opens out into a king-size bed.

While the dining room and bedroom were spaces that naturally suited the bolder wallpapers and fabrics of the decade, the studio demanded a simpler style of decoration. As studios were by their very nature nearly always small, they needed to be functional spaces that could accommodate everything from sleeping to eating. The studio was often used as a workspace too, and as young creatives flocked to big cities their homes also became the places where they painted, designed, wrote and housed fledgling businesses.

It was generally thought that small rooms were unable to accommodate complicated decorative ideas, and magazines such as *House & Garden* recommended that the best way of unifying a concentrated space was to adopt just one colour – whether white, black, orange or whatever – or one pattern throughout. As the studio was generally a space for the young or hard-up, it suited the reasonably priced Scandinavian-style furniture that remained fashionable up until the mid-Sixties. By this stage British companies were beginning to make their own interpretation of this type of furniture, with a far more accessible price point than the Scandinavian imports.

Towards the end of the decade, bright plastic furniture and accessories started appearing in the studio, their gaiety enhanced by the backdrop of white walls. Indeed, white was the wall colour of choice for many Sixties studios: this created a feeling of spaciousness and also offered a practical solution when a studio had to double as a workspace for artists, designers and writers.

'HOUSE & GARDEN LOOKS AT THE POSSIBILITIES OF THE ONE-ROOM LIFE'

AUGUST 1966

Throughout the Sixties, House & Garden *regularly ran features that explored the decorative possibilities of the studio or bedsit. As can be seen from the article overleaf, a studio flat was considered a particularly creative space, either for the young embarking upon their first forays into interior decoration or for artists and designers who lived and worked in a single room.*

Right
A floral-print fabric from John Lewis was used as a curtain to screen off the bed in this studio room from 1966. To the right you can see the oven and kitchen units, and in the foreground are a fold-up dining table and chairs. This scheme was designed for a student.

Far right
A freestanding dividing unit, with shelves and mirrored glass on one side and wardrobes on the other, effectively divides one room into two. The bedspread is from Molylycke, an interiors company with a Scandinavian aesthetic that had opened a showroom in Berners Street, just a few months before this photograph was taken in February 1961.

Below
A picture from 1963 of the artist David
Gentleman's flat, where he lived and
worked. A wall of unpainted wooden
shelves allowed for flexible shelves to
accommodate different-sized books.

'For hundreds of thousands of law-abiding
citizens, the cell is an inescapable way of life.
They must learn to accept the limitations
of one-room living. For many, these cellular
conditions are forbidding, even terrifying.
But for a vast army of young people, their
cells are, paradoxically, escapes into
freedom. For the first time in their lives
they can throw off parental controls and
frustrations. Entering their university rooms
or hostel bed-sitters they feel like jumping
for exuberant joy. For a time, at least, they
will be masters and mistresses of their own
domestic arrangements. To hell with the
adult world! And if social contact is needed,
the companionship of their fellows can be
had on their terms: in the Common Room,
the Debating Hall and on the playing fields.
Unlike the prisoner and the pensioner, the
student and trainee can pick up and put
down loneliness at will. Their ten-by-eight
cells are retreats for working and dreaming.
Above all, they are places for the expression
of their own ideas about the arrangement of
furniture, the use of colour, the decoration of
walls. No longer will any fond mama be able
to exercise her chintzy whim of iron.

But there is usually a fly in most
ointments and here, usually, enters an
official fly. "Issue" furnishings, like "issue"
uniforms, are never right. The inhabitant
of the cell wants to express his or her ideas
and is in no mood for acceptance of ready-
made notions. Yet they have to – until they
get their very own first unfurnished bed-
sitter, whether at home or far from home.
Meantime, they can express their graphic
egos with their own paintings and objets
d'art or near art.

Below left
Every inch of space was used in this all-purpose 1966 room belonging to the industrial designer Carol Russell. To the left is a compact stove, while straight ahead is the cooking area. Canvases and papers are stored wherever there is space, and there is just enough room to also house the artist's dog.

Below right
This sophisticated 1963 room combines a study and a sitting area. The office chair is by Herman Miller and the desk is topped with black Formica. The large teak and leather armchair is by Finn Juhl.

Bottom
This 1964 room set was displayed in Hille's showroom on London's Albemarle Street, and features furniture designed by Michael Green. It shows a smart bedsit intended for a student to work, wash and study in the same small space.

Below
A study fits neatly into the corner of a 1965 room. Saarinen's 'Tulip' chair and the Danish leather chair from Heal's add a Scandinavian note; the walls are covered in a blue-and-white cotton; while a *Royal Pavilion* print by Edward Bawden hangs above the desk.

Right
Tebrax shelving units line the walls of this cheerful 1969 studio room, allowing the occupant to make the most of the restricted space. A red Valiant heater provides additional warmth during the winter months.

'Unless, of course, they are lucky enough to find an unfurnished bed-sitter. Then is the time for true ingenuity. Money is, almost inevitably, in very short supply. That is an accepted thing. Imagination of a high, yet practical, order is required. And, above all, taste.

'But taste, alas, is a subject impossible to teach. In all the hundreds of jobs now advertised for headships and lectureships in Britain's Schools of Art, we never read of a vacancy for an Instructor in Taste.

'The gift – for gift it is – is vouchsafed by the gods in a strictly carefree manner. No merit or training comes into the matter. Four years' instruction in an art school are no guarantee that the student will leave with that tangible but will-o'-the-wisp gift of taste. Yet we have all met the young housewife, quite untrained in subjects of design and decoration, who seems able to transform a room or a house into a composition of gaiety and ingenuity, which has all her friends and acquaintances saying, "I don't know where she gets the knack from, but …"

'All very galling to the bureaucrats and educational planners. Furnishing and decorating a one-room home is probably the most exacting challenge that can be given to any expert. Given a room of say, ten-by-eight, one tenant will put in a camp bed, two chairs and a table and call it a day. Another, borrowing ideas from those masters of compact design, the marine architects, will evolve a shore-based cabin that will give continual visual pleasure to visitors as well as keeping everything ship-shape for the tenant.

'And so it goes on. Given a more grandiloquent interior of, say, thirty-by-twenty, one tenant will produce a comfortless barn of a home; another will make the place a room that entices the eye of the visitor in an irresistible progress, from practical ingenuity to decorative innovation.

'Basically, it's not a question of money. One man can sit behind an eighteenth-century desk carrying the appurtenances of the Man of Distinction, from tooled leather blotter to noble silver-capped ink-well, from *The Economist* diary to the latest *Who's Who*. And it's all as dead as Dean Swift. Another can have a deal trestle-table surmounted by an ancient typewriter, a pile of paperbacks, three clay pipes, two dog-eared box files and pages of notes in the grip of a gigantic paper clip and the whole thing tingles with the vitality and visual interest of Brighton beach on a bank holiday.

'One girl can decorate her bed-sit wall with a well-framed reproduction of a post-Impressionist classic and it's as doleful as a wall in the dentist's waiting room. Another can pin a poster on a cork slab along with twenty art-gallery invitations, ten picture postcards from friends abroad, five reminders to her social self, a torn-out page of a yearned-for dress from *Vogue* or *The Sunday Times* colour magazine and the wall is as gay and colourful as a circus on the village green.'

A RIOT OF FABRIC
THE BEDROOM

'That dreary trio the bedroom suite is now, happily, passé, and the range, in many instances, has taken over. More popular still is the bedroom unit, and the ultimate ideal, now being made by every far-seeing manufacturer, is the modular unit.'

—NOVEMBER 1965

Far left
A 1967 scheme with a very patriotic design. The rounded edges of the bed and the curved shape of the low table that stands next to it reflect how Sixties design tended to use more rounded forms than had been seen in the previous decade.

Left
A four-poster bed from 1966 appears to have wrong-footed this ready-for-bed couple. It is covered in 'Graphics', a Heal's fabric designed by Barbara Brown.

Above
A seriously trendy bedroom was created in the eaves of this Queen's Park, London house in 1967. Walls are wood-panelled and the all-white scheme includes an abundance of sheepskin.

Below
A cane-fronted headboard and a Tang dynasty horse catch the eye in this elegant 1963 bedroom. A wall of mirrored glass covers one wall, while ample storage is afforded by the long row of drawers.

Right
The only colour in this 1966 white room comes from the Hans Tisdall painting and the seat cushions for Eero Saarinen's 'Tulip' chairs. The two white PVC chairs seen in the foreground were from Omk Design.

Following pages
This 1968 bedroom has plenty of Sixties touches, including the crochet bedspread, floral-print canopy and painted cane chairs. The wardrobes and bedside tables are part of the trend for fitted bedroom units that became popular in the Fifties.

At the start of the Sixties, bedroom design was hampered by the way in which furniture was sold. In the same way that the sitting room was blighted by the three-piece suite, so the bedroom was restricted by the trio of dressing table, chest of drawers and wardrobe: three pieces of furniture that were seen as necessary additions to any sleeping area and were typically sold as a matching set. The sheer bulk of these three items meant that by the time they had been crammed into the average bedroom – not forgetting the bed, of course – there wasn't

really any room for decorative flair. This had long been a source of frustration to those with an aesthetic eye but limited means. Companies such as Heal's and the newly founded Habitat began producing slimmer, more stylish alternatives that could be bought individually rather than as a set, and which did not cost a fortune. Habitat was vital in promoting the 'in-store experience', where customers could see the furniture laid out and decide for themselves whether or not it was to their taste, or indeed suitable for their own house. Before this, the

dominance of furniture catalogues meant that customers often had to wait up to 12 weeks for their order to arrive, and when it did, it frequently did not match up to their expectations. As furniture was such a significant investment – often something that was bought only once in a lifetime – it meant that newlyweds might be stuck with a bedroom they hated for the entire duration of their marriage.

Heal's was also the first British firm to produce modular furniture – pieces that were adaptable and could be used alongside

Below
Crochet bedspreads – especially in white – were considered very chic. This 1968 room has walls and curtains in 'Dunbar' by Liberty & Co.

Right
The star of this 1965 room is the wall of shelves with red-lacquered doors. There is even space for a compact dressing table. The strong colour scheme gives the room a unisex appeal.

one other. As fitted units became the norm in kitchens, the same principle began to be used in bedroom planning. By the Sixties, modern kitchens featured high- and low-level cupboards, built in a single unit that ran round the work surfaces, cooker and sink. Similarly, new bedroom designs began to have floor-to-ceiling cupboards that used the wall surfaces to the full. These built-in shelving units were often extended and adapted to incorporate a dressing-table area, a built-in basin or mirror, or even a television. This efficient use of space left the main area of the room clear, uninterrupted by bulky wardrobes or large dressing tables.

The use of pattern was particularly noticeable in the Sixties bedroom. David Hicks, the most influential interior designer of the period, was noted for his bold use of pattern, especially in bedrooms. He would often design a canopied bed with drapes in an identical pattern to that used on the walls and curtains, to create a very unified and smart – yet daring – look. This idea was much copied, and there was a rise in popularity of wallpapers and fabrics that shared the same motifs and colourways.

There was also some thought given to designing the bedroom as a place that encouraged sleep. The rise in the number of prescription sleeping pills that were being doled out in Britain during the Sixties suggested that insomnia was a national problem – a 1967 *House & Garden* article estimated that the total annual number of barbiturates prescribed worked out at 20 tablets a head for the entire population. The same article concluded that if people were doomed to stay awake, however unwillingly, they should at least do so in

Left
The walls, curtains, bed hanging and even the ceiling of this 1967 room were all covered in the same cotton fabric, 'The Pansy' by Sanderson. Note the brightly printed table cover from Liberty, which captures the zeitgeist perfectly, especially as it is topped by a yoga manual.

Below
This boldly curving headboard was dreamed up by *House & Garden*'s decoration editor and built by the in-house photographer. The November 1969 issue predicted that it was 'the 1970 answer to the four-poster bed'. History was against them, but the Indian bedcover enjoyed prolonged popularity well into the next decade.

bedrooms that were as visually pleasurable as possible. There was also a school of thought that suggested that strong colour was soothing rather than stimulating to the brain, which may have encouraged its use in the bedroom. The extended use of a single, vibrant pattern, continued across walls, curtains and bed linen, was thought to create a sense of warmth and harmony. Woodwork and floors were commonly painted white to create a neutral background for the riot of colour that dominated elsewhere.

Canopied beds were also very popular in the smartest bedrooms. In a sense, the Sixties prefigured the craze for the riot of fabric that adorned the Eighties bedroom, with the focal point being a canopied bed upholstered in statement fabrics – except that instead of the floral chintzes that became synonymous with the late-Eighties 'Laura Ashley' look, the Sixties bed was adorned with a bright, small-scale repeat motif that was often Eastern-inspired. The use of the canopy enabled a strong pattern to be used to maximum decorative effect, creating a theatrical statement in the bedroom – especially since there was now space to do so, what with the more efficient designs for clothes storage. In November 1969, the decoration editor of *House & Garden*, Olive Sullivan, designed a modern version of the canopied bed – a single curving sweep of wood built with the aid of one of the magazine's photographers. This very modern, futuristic design went against the grain in that it did not use any fabric whatsoever. 'We think it's the 1970 answer to the four-poster bed. It's been a long time coming, but then, so was penicillin,' declared

Below
A mind-boggling fabric – 'Prism', designed by Wolfgang Bauer for Heal's – covers the walls and bed of this ultra-modern room from 1969. The moulded plastic bed and circular table were designed by Brian Long for the Aeropreen Award 1968 and manufactured by Dunlopillo.

Right
A 1962 child's room using products that were entirely imported from Finland. Note the colourful children's toys that were imported by Stockmann/Orno.

Far right
Flea-market finds and an assortment of posters, photographs and album covers decorate this 1969 bedroom belonging to a young Parisian artist.

Right below
Modular rosewood furniture shapes this 1963 bedroom. The cabinets and other pieces were designed by a shipbuilding

firm, and so make the most effective use of the available space.

Far right below
Pale blue abounds in this 1966 bedroom: the striking pelmet adds definition to the four-poster bed, and shutters take the place of curtains.

the accompanying article. Sadly it didn't catch on, and the four-poster played less of a role in Seventies bedroom design.

The Sixties bedroom had radically changed from its Fifties predecessor. Although Scandinavian – or Scandinavian-style – furniture was still popular, the overall aesthetic had changed. Italian design had ushered in furniture of a more curving, sensuous nature that was usually made in darker or lacquered wood. This fostered a different look from the one created by the blond-wood designs that were so typical of the Fifties. Built-in units spelt the end for bulky wardrobes, while a growing tide of romanticism brought in dramatic, bold patterns that were used on wallpaper and fabrics alike. Ethnic designs competed with the influence of Art Nouveau, which found its way into the swirling, organic shapes that tied in so well with the psychedelic trend that grew as the decade advanced. By the late Sixties, bedrooms had become a space where imagination was really allowed to run riot, whether in a profusion of pattern or in the playful influence of Pop art.

Following pages
Alphonse Mucha prints set the scene for this psychedelic purple bedroom from 1966, which shows how the art-nouveau aesthetic was being reinvented in a very Sixties way, complete with an unusual mirrored ceiling. The inclusion of furniture upholstered in black leather continues the room's Sixties update.

LUXURY & REFUGE
THE BATHROOM

'The bathroom is now teetering on the edge, so to speak, of becoming the most civilised room in the house. And why not? Here, of all places, you are most likely to be left in peace. At a desperate pinch you can lock yourself in with a good book. After all, you can always pretend to be having a bath. Meanwhile, there you are, where all is warm and scented, with that good book and, of course, a drink.'

—JUNE 1967

Left
Wooden shutters cast patterned shafts of light across a 1968 bathroom in Chelsea. The carpeted floor and painted Swedish dresser imbue this bathing area with the atmosphere of a living room.

Above
In 1962, the owners of this cottage in East Anglia created a bold look in their new upstairs bathroom, covering bath and walls in a yellow-and-red French paisley patterned wallpaper from Cole & Son.

Left
A wallpaper from Cole & Son mimics the effect of tiles in a 1965 scheme. In the bedroom beyond stand a pair of scrubbed oak dressing tables from Gomme.

Below
Floor-to-ceiling Italian mosaic tiles create a striking scheme in a 1968 bathroom. A wool carpet in golden yellow adds warmth – the accompanying article stated that 'in the bathroom, of all rooms, a carpet is a necessity'.

Left
Judging from this man's expression, these late-Sixties his 'n' hers bathtubs were not all they were cracked up to be. Still, the floor cheers things up a bit – the carpet is called 'Tulip' and was designed by Bernat Klein. The Italian sofa is upholstered in vinyl, hence its extreme shininess.

Below
Painted white floorboards and waterproof wallpaper from Cole & Son create an extremely stylish 1967 bathroom that makes a feature out of an awkward attic space.

The bathroom was fast becoming not just a place of luxury but also one of refuge. As open-plan living became popular, the bathroom was increasingly seen as a welcome escape, a haven where you could shut yourself away from the rest of the family. At the top end of the market, bathrooms continued the trend for opulent excess first seen in the Thirties. Sophie Anstey, the author of the article quoted on page 91, seems to have experienced more than her fair share of super-opulent bathrooms, as she revealed later on in the same piece: 'I have even taken after-dinner coffee in the bathroom of one American hostess. Very comfortable (on little bergères covered in a pretty toile to match the walls) after the initial shock of realising that we were going to be there for a good hour or more.'

While it is extremely unlikely that this particular after-dinner ritual ever caught on, it does show that the bathroom was beginning to be a room where interiors trends were followed and displayed, as opposed to a spartan place of sanitation. Tiles – both on the floor and on walls – were popular and were used to create opulent and dramatic effects. The most coveted tiles came from Spain, France and Italy. Spanish manufacturers tended to produce mostly traditional tiles, while Italian tiles were much more daring in their scope, being manufactured in jewel-rich glazes and adorned with cursive, filigree patterns, as well as making new versions of traditional motifs. French tiles tended to be more restrained and had a 'prettier' look, and were used to create delicate, feminine interiors. France was also the main source

Below
This bathroom at Stowe Castle in
Buckinghamshire combined tradition
with modernity in this 1967 image.
An antique chest of drawers, Corinthian
pillars and a marble bust are offset by the
turquoise floor and cobalt walls.

Right
This late-Sixties bathroom in a neo-
Georgian house in Chelsea also uses
different shades of blue to striking effect.
The twin basins are decorated with a gold
motif that is also used on the bath and
bidet seen reflected in the mirror above.

Far right
This 1967 bathroom is completely
covered in mosaic, including the shelf
that tops the lavatory cistern and the
surround of the basin.

of terracotta tiles, which could be used in bathrooms as well as kitchens. Classic Dutch tiles were popular too, especially those hand-painted at Makkum, where a factory had been manufacturing tiles for over three hundred years. As for flooring, carpets were occasionally laid, but this was rightly seen as a somewhat impractical choice. Marble was also a popular, luxurious option, although the sheer weight of the heavy tiles made them difficult to lay if the bathroom was not at the bottom of the house, and they were cold underfoot.

Below
A 1964 image of Terence and Caroline Conran's bathroom in Fitzroy Square. Tongue-and-groove walls are painted white, the floor is covered in cork tiles and the blind is in a pink-and-red Conran fabric.

Right
This picture-lined room evokes the feel of a hallway with its L-shape and its carpeted floor.

Far right
A vinyl wallcovering from Crown mimics the effect of blue-and-white tiles.

Right below
A *trompe-l'œil* effect: Italian tiles above the basin contrast with a tile-patterned waterproof wallcovering from Cole & Son in front of it.

Far right below
A wood-panelled bathroom incorporates plenty of storage. All pictures on this page are from 1967.

Tiles aside, pine was a common wallcovering during this decade, especially for bathrooms with a more Scandinavian, clean-cut aesthetic. Mirrored walls were also used to maximize light and space, although prospective redecorators were cautioned against installing multiple mirrored walls – 'or you will see yourself, fragmented, over and over again, wherever you look'. Plastic was also often used as a wallcovering, particularly in the form of waterproof vinyl wallpapers in bright patterns. At the time this was seen as being rather forward-looking, especially as Pop art began to influence interior design in the mid- to late Sixties.

In technical terms, one of the most notable changes in bathroom design during the Sixties was the advent of mixer taps. These became increasingly common, as did showers – either separate shower units placed over the bath or else freestanding showers or wet rooms. Unlike the Fifties, when shower units were marketed as a lifetime investment – something that you would take with you when you moved house – in the Sixties they had become part of the fixed bathroom design.

As in the rest of the house, the cooler tones of the early Sixties suites gave way first of all to white, and then to colours such as avocado – the harbinger of the coloured bathroom suites of the Seventies. Lavatory fittings took on a more coherent appearance, with close-coupled designs and new plastic seats that could be made in the same shade as the bathroom suite. The bath was generally set in a corner and panelled in, although as the Sixties progressed it was sometimes adventurously set on a central

Below
Bathroom designers were exploring
new ways of laying out rooms – this 1963
example functions as a wet room, as the
floor slopes down to the shower area.
The bath – not seen here – is also sunken.

Below left
Amazingly, this elaborate 1963 bathroom was on a yacht. Blue-and-white mosaic surrounds the bath and basin, while additional decoration is provided by the eighteenth-century Chinese panels.

Below centre
Bulls' horns and marble-effect wallpaper add drama to a 1963 Italian bathroom.

Below right
This Bayswater bathroom created quite an impact in 1964 with its wall of circular-patterned tiles in gold and white.

dais. Victorian roll-top baths, especially the claw-footed variety, also made a comeback towards the end of the decade. At the luxury end of the spectrum, baths designed by Godfrey Bonsack were considered the ultimate mark of sophistication. As the trend for having the same pattern throughout a room took off, Godfrey Bonsack was also the go-to company to re-create this look in the bathroom – it could take the fabric of your choice and imprint it on to fibreglass baths and basins, so that they perfectly matched the walls or curtains.

Concealed plumbing also helped hugely in terms of creating a stylish bathroom interior, and was particularly useful for bathrooms that needed to be fitted into small spaces. Ugly pipes could be set into the wall, and more innovative designers put forward designs for 'floating' lavatories and basins that were fixed directly to the wall, without any need for a supporting pedestal. According to various accounts in *House & Garden*, there were unforeseen practical obstacles to consider, however: much time seems to have been spent in cajoling reluctant plumbers to install these futuristic bathroom fittings.

Less controversial was the trend for basins placed within fitted bathroom units. This allowed for extra storage space both underneath the basin and on the countertop to either side of it. Then as now, these counters were often topped with marble, slate or ceramic, or more economically with Formica or other types of treated plastic.

Tying in with the fashion for integrating the bathroom decoration with that of the rest of the house, it also became standard practice to hang paintings or prints in the bathroom – made possible by advances in ventilation. At the end of the Sixties, stylish bathrooms had become treasure troves of rich colour, pattern and decorative touches. Little wonder that they were becoming the go-to place of escape for those looking for a peaceful oasis when the rest of the house felt too crowded.

2. HOUSES

104

'MONOCHROME MODERN'

CASE STUDY | DECEMBER 1964

108

'ARTIST'S RETREAT'

CASE STUDY | DECEMBER 1964

114

'A GOTHIC REVIVAL'

CASE STUDY | MAY 1965

134

'A TOUCH OF THEATRE'

CASE STUDY | MAY 1967

138

'BIBA AT HOME'

CASE STUDY | FEBRUARY 1968

144

'MADE FOR THE MOMENT'

CASE STUDY | NOVEMBER 1966

162

'MUSIC & MAYHEM'

CASE STUDY | SEPTEMBER 1968

166

'UNIVERSITY CHALLENGE'

CASE STUDY | SEPTEMBER 1969

118

'CAFÉ CULTURE'

122

'NEW ROOTS'

130

'PAST PERFECT'

148

'OF SOUKS & SPICES'

152

'WHITE CUBE'

158

'SHIP-SHAPE'

MONOCHROME MODERN

CASE STUDY | DECEMBER 1964

Bridget Riley was one of the best-known British artists of the Sixties, her monochrome Op art canvases tapping into the fresh, innovative zeitgeist of the decade. In 1964 she was living in a flat on the top floor of an Edwardian terrace in Earls Court, which comprised just two rooms, one of which she kept as a 'well-disciplined and well-designed junk room'.

Left
In a corner of the studio was a white work table where Riley produced her paintings: the table was designed for her by fellow artist Peter Sedgley.

Right
The artist at work in her attic studio in Earls Court.

Riley worked, ate and slept in this one
room. Walls and floorboards were
painted white not because it was
fashionable, but to provide a neutral
background for working out designs.

This 'junk room' contained various cuts and
lengths of hardboard, canvases, paintings
and other odds and ends relating to Riley's
work. The other room was used as a multi-
purpose studio: a place where she slept, lived
and worked.

The studio made quite an impact owing
to its sheer whiteness. The floorboards were
painted white, as were the walls, with the
remains of a broad band of pale grey-green
that ran above the cornice. Riley deliberately
left this band as a contrast, to emphasize the
whiteness of everything else. The only touch
of colour was a print of an apple from a
commercial poster, stuck on the wall beside
the bed, made up of russet and golden tints.

Riley was a firm believer in the virtues of a
white background. 'I like the light it brings,'
she said, 'and it helps me to think. … I'm sure
the background of white often helps me sort
things out.' Even her enormous work table
was white. This highly practical unit was
designed for her by Peter Sedgley, another
artist preoccupied with the possibilities of
black and white. The table was very large
and beautifully balanced: it could be raised
to different heights, could seat a crowd
for dinner and could even be stood and
sawn on, for Riley's experiments in design
sometimes needed considerable space and a
wide range of materials.

The only contrast to this whiteness, apart
from the apple poster, was the broad black-
and-white checks of a gingham bedspread,
a present from her mother, and a couple of
black chairs. There was also a Norwegian
Anglepoise-style lamp in grey. This simple,
bare atelier had a decorative quality that
perfectly reflected the taste and artistic
aesthetic of its talented occupant.

ARTIST'S RETREAT

The Scottish abstract painter Alan Davie converted the stable block of a Queen Anne house in Hertfordshire into a studio and home for himself and his wife and daughter. A decade on, he substantially extended it, almost doubling its size: the results are shown here.

Above

The stable block's new extension included a large conservatory with a bedroom above it.

Right

The artist's bright canvases added vivacity to the dining area, which was located in the original hayloft. You can also spot the artist's two poodles and a corner of the cage of his jazz-loving, talking parrot. A teak drop-leaf table is surrounded by teak and cane chairs.

Below
Off the new conservatory was the sitting
room, complete with a grand piano and
one of Arne Jacobsen's 'Egg' chairs.

Right
Davie pictured in his new studio,
surrounded by his paint pots. The artist
tended to work on several paintings at the
same time.

Left
A large Japanese fish, made of paper, hung in the conservatory. The room was filled with red geraniums and the tiled floor was covered with vibrant Persian rugs and kilims.

Below
A close-up of the shelves in the main bedroom, which were filled with a collection of curios.

Davie converted his former studio into a sitting room, and added a spacious new studio on to the side of the house. He also added a garden room with a new bedroom above it.

The new garden room, or conservatory, was divided from the sitting room by folding doors and was filled with a mass of vegetation. This was typical of the whole house – each room flowed into the others, all ablaze with colour. The interiors also underwent a considerable transformation – whenever a new painting went up on the wall, everything was switched around.

Colour was everywhere, not just in Davie's canvases and sketches on the walls, but in all the various objects around the house. He also delighted in pattern. The sitting room floor was covered with a bright yellow carpet, but the garden room opening off it had a more practical tiled floor, covered with kilim and Persian rugs. The garden room lived up to its name with the masses of vermilion geraniums that were packed into it. Amid these, beside the never-closed doors into the sitting room, stood a stout leather elephant from Liberty. Curtains were grey-and-white striped Welsh flannel lined in red.

Up the open staircase, past a mural painted by Davie himself, was an open-plan sitting area. A large oblong dining table provided a focal point, as did the wildlife – this bohemian set-up was also home to a yellow canary and a green-and-yellow parrot. The white walls displayed groups of objects such as Mexican wands in bright wools and stars of feathers and straw. On the shelves were arrangements of small

Mexican wooden animals and miniature furniture, flints and sea-weathered roots. Off this sitting room were the kitchen and an adjacent bathroom. The kitchen walls were painted in bright shades of red and yellow gloss, and the floor was red. Everything in the tiny kitchen was within arm's reach and the custom-built units were all made by Davie.

More treasures of this kind were to be found in the main bedroom. Here, the walls and floor were white, with interest provided by large paintings – and another leather elephant. The house was described as having a creative, transitory atmosphere, where nothing was in a fixed position, but rather there was the constant possibility of alteration and change.

A GOTHIC REVIVAL

CASE STUDY | MAY 1965

A striking example of Regency Gothic Revival architecture, set amid the Wicklow Mountains in Ireland, Luggala Lodge had been completely restored and modernized by Oonagh Guinness, daughter of Ernest Guinness (himself brother of the present Earl of Iveagh). When the house accidentally burned down in January 1956 she had it rebuilt exactly as before, enlisting the help of the Dublin architect Alan Hope.

Far left
With walls, carpet and chair fabric in varying hues of lilac, this bedroom retained a period feel while making the most of an up-to-the-minute paint colour.

Above left
Interior decorator John Hill had the 'Rose and Lace' paper by Edward Bawden custom-printed in candy pink to match this bedroom's colour scheme.

Below left
As with the bedroom, this wallpaper was printed in a bespoke colourway. This is a Gothic Revival paper by Cole & Son that was originally designed for the Houses of Parliament, dating from about 1860.

Desmond FitzGerald, 29th Knight of Glin and former president of the Irish Georgian Society, wrote of the unusual house: 'It is that special brand of eighteenth-century gothick that rejoices in little battlements, trefoil and quatrefoil windows and ogee mantelpieces: in fact, the gothick of pastrycooks and Rockingham china. Somehow this whitewashed toy pavilion fits into its green-grey setting of old twisted oak trees, beeches, mossy rocks and mountains in the most unnaturally natural way. Its very unlikelihood carries it off with a vivid panache, whereas a more contrived rustic house, such as a nineteenth-century architect might have built in such a spot, would have had the appearance of utter banality.'

Now married to her third husband, Oonagh Ferreras also embarked on the process of re-creating the interiors, aided by the designer John Hill, of Green & Abbott, a company based in London's Hanover Square. In his *House & Garden* feature, Desmond FitzGerald wrote: 'Today the interior, with its elaborate wallpapers, chandeliers and plush comfort, is more early Victorian in feeling than Georgian, but the hospitality and gaiety of the house is very much more evocative of the eighteenth than of the nineteenth century.' However, the bright patterned wallpapers and the bold colour schemes – along with the walnut and mahogany furniture – exemplified the Victorian revival trend that appeared in fashionable houses towards the end of the decade, and reflected the contemporary style of the Sixties in a way that its new owner had, presumably, never even intended.

Left above
The hall retained its original Gothic chimneypiece, while the geometric 'Periwinkle' wallpaper by Edward Bawden added a touch of the Sixties.

Left below
This bedroom exuded a strong Victorian feel, thanks to the chintzy 'Lilac Terrace' wallpaper from Cole & Son.

Below
Unlike the hall, the chimneypiece in the drawing room was destroyed in the fire – its replacement was in a completely different style. Above it hung a painting by René Magritte.

CAFÉ CULTURE

CASE STUDY | DECEMBER 1965

The owners of this London flat were a Canadian–English couple, Michael and Sheila Van Bloemen, who set up one of the first coffee shops in London, the Troubadour on the Old Brompton Road. They had conceived the idea 11 years previously when they were honeymooning in Amsterdam, where coffee houses were atmospheric and furnished with well-worn, rough-hewn antiques.

Right
An assortment of oddments was arranged upon an old oak chest. The cut-out paper ships that hung above it were originally part of a puppet theatre.

Far right
In the dining area, a cluster of pictures was arranged on the peacock-blue wall – a mixture of reproductions, primitive flower paintings by John Deacon and a painting of a traction engine by A W Chesher. The large horse came from a fairground and the dining chairs are reproductions of a William Morris design by Dunn's of Bromley.

Below
The sitting room fireplace was simply a hole in the wall, underlined by a shelf and a stack of logs. An assortment of vintage items decorated the area, along with a portrait of Queen Mary by John Deacon.

Right
The attic housed a television room. The mural on the window was painted by a friend of the couple.

Centre right
The dining table is laid with Spanish pottery from Casa Pupo, Mexican mats and glasses, and an arrangement of paper poppies.

Far right
A leather chesterfield and other seats were grouped near the fireplace. In a former incarnation, the oak coffee table was used as a pig slaughtering block.

At that time, the only coffee bars in London were mock Italian, decorated with Mediterranean scenes wreathed in plastic grapes on rickety trellises, and equipped with Italian espresso coffee machines.

The Van Bloemens' coffee shop was furnished with church pews as seats and Victorian sewing machines converted into tables (a new idea then), plus a collection of antique musical instruments to justify its name. Over time, the energetic couple gradually collected more instruments, coffee grinders, coffee pots and weighing machines that spilled out of the café and into their three-storey flat above. Their own home revealed the full extent of their passion for collecting: items included old money banks, bird cages, toys and tobacco jars.

Although they bought things for their visual merit rather than for their rarity or value, they amassed a decent collection of folk art and country furniture. As they had three small children, this sturdy furniture suited their lifestyle. The pine and cane dining chairs were made by Dunn's of Bromley to a William Morris design; elsewhere were Hebridean straw chairs. The overall atmosphere channelled that of an informal (and rather eccentric) Victorian country house.

The eclectic assortment of folk art and curios was given order by clever arrangements. A busy wall of pictures, or of brightly coloured antique wooden puppets, was offset by a calm expanse of plain white wall, a mirror or a patch of natural wooden floor. The only exception was the attic, which was kept comparatively bare, lined with low seats and painted a mustard yellow. There was one dramatic decorative flourish, however: a window painted with Pre-Raphaelite–inspired romantic motifs.

NEW ROOTS

CASE STUDY | SEPTEMBER 1963

Today the Beth Chatto Gardens near Elmstead Market in Essex is famous for its clever planting of the tricky terrain. The seeds of this innovative garden were planted in 1960, when Beth Chatto and her horticulturist husband, Andrew, decided to move from their house in Colchester to an unkempt patch of land close to the family fruit farm.

Left
Steps led down from the entrance hall to the open-plan dining and kitchen area. The split-level space made each element of the living area feel like a separate room.

Right
The kitchen and dining area ran into the lower-level sitting area, which had French windows that opened on to the garden.

Following pages
Another view of the sitting area. The kitchen is just visible to the right.

Left
In the dining area, Utility chairs from Ercol surrounded a simple wooden table. A floor-to-ceiling window provided a good view of the garden.

Below left
A unit of open shelves let through light while partially screening off the kitchen from the dining area. The unit also doubled as a food-preparation area.

Below right
From the entrance hall, it is possible to see the different levels of the open-plan living area.

Bottom
A view of the dining area and the hall beyond it, from the sitting area. The dividing unit incorporated storage cupboards, bookshelves and an 'Agavector' heater.

After 20 years of commuting between Colchester and Elmstead Market Beth and Andrew Chatto knew exactly what kind of house they wanted to build. They commissioned the Essex-based architect Bryan Thomas to design a modern farmhouse that would blend into the local landscape. The feel of a farmhouse was evoked through the low-pitched roof and whitewashed exterior walls. Inside, natural materials were used where possible. The entrance hall was timber clad, the tiled floors were of stone, hardwood or cork, and the sitting room ceiling was tongue-and-groove timber.

At the heart of the house was the large open-plan space that combined sitting room, dining room and living area into one big space. The sloping ceiling and the floor levels, staggered at different heights, served

Below and bottom
These two bedrooms, located next to each other, were identical in size and similarly decorated. They belonged to the Chattos' two daughters.

Right above
The back door opened on to a paved courtyard around which the outbuildings were grouped – a modern take on a traditional farmyard.

Right below
The living area overlooked a pond that the Chattos had channelled and reshaped. The raised room in the roof was Andrew's attic study, reached via an external staircase.

to break up the space and allowed it to be open-plan without feeling too cavernous. There was a freestanding shelving unit which separated the cooking area from the dining area, while a sideboard divided the dining area from the slightly sunken sitting room. Placed at the heart of the sitting area was an enormous open fireplace with a wide raised hearth, which maintained the comforting feel of a traditional farmhouse.

At the other side of the house was a cluster of four bedrooms and a bathroom. The two children's bedrooms were identical in size and incorporated plenty of built-in storage. And continuing the intriguing use of different levels, Andrew Chatto's study was to be found in an attic room situated above the kitchen and accessed via an external staircase.

Throughout, the house was simply furnished, although more furniture was due to be added. These photographs show a new building, at a time when the Chattos were still in the process of adding the finishing touches to the interiors.

Having chosen to build their house on a wasteland deemed unsuitable for farming and covered in briars and blackthorn, the couple knew that creating a garden was going to be difficult. They sought out specialist plants and subdivided the garden into different areas in order to work with the idiosyncrasies of the plot. The result was a masterpiece in the cultivation of challenging terrain, as the Chattos sought out a diverse range of unusual plants that were suitable for the various conditions. This inspired them to set up the Beth Chatto Gardens nursery in 1967, and Beth Chatto went on to publish eight books on gardening, starting

with *The Dry Garden* in 1978. Although it is the gardens that draw the visitors, the adjoining house is a fantastic example of a Sixties building in which modern design has been carefully tailored to a rural aesthetic.

PAST PERFECT

CASE STUDY | FEBRUARY 1961

This spacious stuccoed London house belonged to the politician John Profumo and his wife, the actress Valerie Hobson. Its traditional decoration shows a different side to the Sixties – of opulent interiors firmly rooted in the past instead of reflecting current trends.

With its Regency architecture and impressively large drawing room, this Regent's Park house drew on classic French decoration to create a very traditional effect. As the home of the then minister of state for war John Profumo and his actress wife, Valerie Hobson – who starred in a number of films from the Thirties to the Fifties, including *Werewolf in London* (1935), *Great Expectations* (1946) and *Kind Hearts and Coronets* (1949) – it was used as a space for frequent entertaining and needed therefore to be formal.

The stone-flagged entrance hall was painted green, with *trompe-l'œil* decorations by the set designer and artist Martin Battersby. Off the hall was an ante-room, decorated by the French interior designer Stéphane Boudin. At this time, Boudin had

been commissioned by Jacqueline Kennedy to work on the renovation of the White House – he was one of the most foremost interior decorators of the day.

At the centre of the house was the 12m- (40ft-) long drawing room, painted in pale ivory with plaster medallions on either side of the room's two chimney breasts. The room was dominated by a huge Aubusson carpet, with a design of pink flowers on a green background. Two large oil paintings, bought by Hobson from an old French chateau, completed the effect.

However, in the article, Hobson confessed to 'a near-secret desire to hang her Matthew Smiths and Graham Sutherlands on the walls of this handsome Regency room'. Her remark reveals the different attitude to interior design in the Sixties –

there was a far greater division between traditional and modern in formal schemes than there is today. As you can see from the images, there is very little in these rooms to reference the Sixties – or indeed the twentieth century.

Still, timeless as the rooms might look, this particular period was a turbulent one for the Profumos. Four months after this feature was published, Profumo met the 19-year-old model Christine Keeler at a party at Cliveden and began an affair with her. Despite it lasting only a few weeks, Keeler's simultaneous relationship with a Russian official meant that, given Britain's uneasy relationship with the Soviet Union, the Profumo Affair became a major security incident and the scandal culminated in Profumo's resignation from politics.

A TOUCH OF THEATRE

CASE STUDY | MAY 1967

This large, modern flat in the heart of Mayfair was entirely redecorated for the actor Peter Sellers and his wife, the actress Britt Ekland. Sellers commissioned a pair of decorators, Franco Nadali and Stewart Richmond Black, to decorate the flat, making additions to the decorators' plans himself. This, along with Ekland's taste for Swedish style – pale colours and modern furniture – meant that the final design was very much a collaborative one.

Left
A curtain of patterned white-and-black silk from the US textiles firm David and Dash set a bold tone in the sitting area. The seating includes a Mies van der Rohe 'Barcelona' chair and a lounge chair by Tobia Scarpa.

Right
Britt Ekland's dressing room was lined with floor-to-ceiling louvred doors, which concealed her dressing table, clothes and extensive shoe collection

Below
Looking towards the sitting room past the bathroom: the pale-grey carpet used throughout the apartment was custom dyed. The living room doors – like the rest of the panelled room – were stained turquoise, with the moulding picked out in gold.

Below right
The L-shaped living room: at the back are a 'Tulip' dining table and armchairs by Eero Saarinen, while the tile-topped coffee table in the sitting area was made by Christopher Bateman.

The flat's flooring had been the first topic of discussion, with the designers wanting white marble, Ekland keen on white carpeting, and Sellers eventually deciding that both were impractical and opting for pale grey instead. Indeed, Sellers had strong opinions on the flat's decoration – he went for mostly modern furniture and was very keen on ceramics: the ceramic tiles for the coffee table in the living room were specially designed by Stewart Black, who also created the wall panel that concealed the television. The flat was kitted out with the latest technology, including a cutting-edge hi-fi system incorporating both wireless and tape recorder.

Their son's room had walls covered in pale-brown hessian, with a stripped-pine desk, while the bedspread, curtains and one wall were all in a similar striped linen. The girls' room was more feminine, with a French wallpaper and matching curtains of green and blue flowers on white. The floor was white vinyl. The main bathroom was small, with a mirrored wall to create a feeling of space. The other walls were covered in a putty-coloured mosaic, with a mosaic frieze in white, brown and putty. Ekland's dressing room had concertina-louvred doors from floor to ceiling, which were carefully placed to conceal her dressing table – and her extensive collection of shoes.

BIBA AT HOME

CASE STUDY | FEBRUARY 1968

When Barbara Hulanicki opened the first Biba shop in Kensington Church Street in 1964, it was an instant hit with a generation of young shoppers. Her Edwardian house in Kensington, where she lived with her husband, Stephen Fitz-Simon, was as full of decorative notions and explosive colours as the shop.

Left
Faux fur cushions were heaped on a gold ottoman in the drawing room.

Above
Barbara Hulanicki reflected in the mirror of an Edwardian nursery washstand.

Right
Lamps concealed in tall vases lit a corner of the dark drawing room. The velvets, gilt ceiling and ornate mirror created a richly opulent effect.

Below
A beaded curtain screened off the dining room, which had a peacock-blue and green colour scheme.

Right
An attention-grabbing wallpaper by Julie Hodgess contrasted with the plain, stripped-pine furniture in the kitchen.

Below
In the main bedroom, walls and soft furnishings were all in a single cotton dress fabric from Biba.

Right above
The nursery had a sophisticated colour scheme, predominantly cream and yellow ochre with vivid pink accents.

Far right above
A perforated screen, painted the same shade of mauve as the walls and woodwork, helped create privacy in the bathroom.

Right below
A brass bedstead, found in the Portobello Road, stands in the spare bedroom, decorated in another Biba cotton.

In the Kensington house, as in the Biba shop, the scene was set with stagey lighting, aspidistras in baroque jardinières and a good supply of mirrors. And the decoration likewise was the product of the collaboration between Barbara Hulanicki and artist-designer Julie Hodgess.

At the heart of the house was the main bedroom, with a dressing room and bathroom opening off it. The dressing room was as exuberant as Hulanicki's boutiques, with a bright-pink and mauve colour scheme, and a carpet of yellow ochre – the carpets throughout the house were in the same colour.

Hulanicki's son's room was located on the top floor, enlivened by a flock of yellow toy birds. She made the decision to decorate it using strong colour, from the bold wallpaper to the Parma violet of the cot cover.

In the drawing room, the walls were covered in a gold floral design against a brown ground; the ceiling was sprayed with gold paint to continue the theme. The high ceiling in the dining room was painted in a dark shade to emphasize its height, a clever trick that looked particularly striking at night. It took six coats of paint to get the dining room walls the correct shade of peacock blue, with further flamboyant touches appearing in the form of peacock feathers, a coloured-bead curtain, a Tiffany lamp suspended above the circular table and a tablecloth made out of green baize.

Artificial lighting was kept deliberately soft, mimicking the effect of gaslight. Natural light was diffused with screens of fine mesh battened on to the windows. Even more shade was provided by the large Moorish-inspired screen in the drawing room.

Barbara Hulanicki's interest in Art Nouveau was the key to the whole mood of her home. 'It's a stimulating period of design to surround oneself with – in clothes and in interior design,' she says. 'And although it's now vulgarized all over the place, it can never become banal to me. Indoors, the elements of the style can produce real warmth and nostalgia, which I find bewitching, and, of course, it's all a trifle decadent. All in all, it's a fashion it's possible to explore and exploit without spending a lot of money. And it's certainly got glamour. Of what other styles can you say all that?'

MADE FOR THE MOMENT

CASE STUDY | NOVEMBER 1966

Bright colour, beige walls and a psychedelic wall made of coloured glass: this terraced house in central London clearly belongs to the Swinging Sixties. The bold decoration reflects the outgoing personality of its owner, the American socialite John Galliher.

Right
The main bedroom was furnished with a writing desk and comfortable armchair, along with a collection of curios.

Far right
The Sixties trend for cheese plants saw these easy-to-maintain houseplants find their way into a huge number of interiors. This pair in the sitting room foreground required no maintenance at all, since they were made of brass. The sofa is covered in beige fur and flanked by a pair of Mies van der Rohe stools.

Below left
A large terracotta figure, dating from 1890, reclined against a mirror wall in the sitting room.

Below right
Vintage textiles made for a colourful bedcover and stool in the main bedroom, while Pop art pieces enlivened the walls.

Bottom
A corner of the kitchen with its compact dining table – beyond it is the garden, with an Emilio Greco statue peering in at the window.

Right
The wall at one end of the sitting room was covered with thick glass panels by the artist Michael Haynes – this close-up shot shows the depth of these backlit 'constructions'.

This house in Belgravia might have been small, but it resonated with Sixties style. It belonged to the socialite John Galliher, whose winning personality brought him an impressive array of famous friends. As a young man in Beverly Hills, by chance he ran into the interior decorator Elsie de Wolfe. Having heard that he was new to the town, she asked him whether there was anyone he would like to meet. Greta Garbo, he replied, and she arranged it. Garbo went on to become a friend of Galliher, who, when he subsequently moved to Paris, became acquainted with everyone from Gertrude Stein to the Duke and Duchess of Windsor.

By nature he was restless, moving around a lot. Two of his previous flats – one in Paris, the other in London – had already been shown in *House & Garden* by the time that this Belgravia house was featured. His talent in interior decoration was to upend all the normal conventions of design and decoration, while at the same time creating a comfortable room that felt homely as well as avant-garde.

This Chester Row terrace house previously had a narrow hall and small rooms. Galliher gutted the ground floor, so that the front door opened straight into one large room. At the far end of this was a wall covered in glass panels by Michael Haynes. The effect was part stained-glass window and part kaleidoscopic tribute to Pop art. For contrast, the walls were painted a subdued shade of dark beige, giving the room an evening feel and emphasizing the bright furniture, zebra-print rug and modern paintings by Rufino Tamayo, Maurice Brianchon, David Badd and Aika.

Other rooms in this small house were similarly unusual and imaginative, combining a mix of inexpensive curios and more valuable pieces. The kitchen and dining room had a brown-and-white scheme, with walls papered in a geometric print, while the tablecloth and curtains were of coarse hessian sackcloth. Painted in bright red, the rush-seated dining chairs added a shot of colour to the otherwise two-toned room. The kitchen looked out on to the paved garden.

Upstairs, the bedrooms were equally engaging, with Pop art paintings, bright textiles and an eclectic mix of antiques and ornaments. This was just one of John Galliher's many houses, but it had the character of a home that had been carefully constructed over decades – a reflection of the larger-than-life personality of its owner.

OF SOUKS & SPICES

CASE STUDY | JULY 1961

Morocco was the place to be in the Sixties. Seven small houses near the kasbah in Tangier were transformed into a sumptuous house that captured the imagination of the fabulously wealthy heiress Barbara Hutton.

Left
The cluster of houses was hidden behind a heavy door in the middle of the kasbah.

Above
The paved terrace, decorated with mosaic benches and a profusion of flowers.

Right
In the formal salon, the sofa was covered with an Indian fabric and jewelled cushions that were hand-embroidered with gold thread.

Left
In a second-floor sitting room, an eighteenth-century Japanese screen dominated the wall. The carpet was modern and sourced in Tangier.

Below left
The main bedroom had creamy pink walls and a coral bedspread. The headboard was made to a traditional Moorish decorative pattern.

Below right
The Blue Room was a mishmash of different inspirations – English ship's furniture, a modern carpet, a Venetian chandelier and a mirror from Fez.

Woolworths heiress Barbara Hutton was known for her seven marriages, party-fuelled lifestyle and spectacular spending habits, so any house that she occupied was guaranteed to be extraordinary.

In the mid-Fifties, Hutton bought a large house in the middle of the Tangier kasbah, near to the Grand Socco, the old marketplace. The house had been constructed from a series of seven small vernacular buildings that had been linked together by the former owner.

Hutton continued the work of the former occupant in turning the cluster of disparate houses into a single, substantial villa with modern comforts, but the results of the unusual conversion could still be seen in the completely bewildering layout of the house. It was laid out across a number of different levels, and had such a confusing effect upon first-time visitors that they often ended up going round in circles.

The flat roof was an attraction in its own right, consisting of a series of terraces, painted in blue and white and crenellated. From this vantage point, it was possible to look out over the whole kasbah to the Atlantic stretching out beyond it – a beguiling contrast to the fact that the house opened directly off the narrow, dark streets of the marketplace.

The first floor contained an opulent bedroom, known as the Blue Room thanks to its vibrant hues, a living room and Hutton's own suite. Her bedroom was sumptuously decorated in yellows and corals, with ornate embroidered fabrics and rugs sourced in Morocco. From the Blue Room, a small landing opened on to the staircase that led up to the terraced rooftops.

Aside from the roof, the large patio – accessed via French windows in the summer dining room – provided an oasis of tranquillity away from the bustle of the city. Here mosaic benches were arranged around verdant flower beds and a gnarled old fig tree that produced an abundance of fruit. In the heart of one of North Africa's most vibrant cities, Hutton had managed to create that rarest of gems – an urban retreat filled with both greenery and silence.

WHITE CUBE

CASE STUDY | NOVEMBER 1967

During the Sixties the architect and furniture designer Max Clendinning created flat-pack furniture that reflected the decade's love for innovative forms. Pictured here are his house in Islington and his Belfast studio – both of which reflected Clendinning's individual style.

Left
All the furniture in the London sitting room was designed by Max Clendinning. The eau-de-nil shape on the wall rose up to form a large circle on the ceiling.

Above
In the study, the bolsters on the divan were covered with yellow canvas to match the walls, while the sides of the armchair were painted with bright murals.

Previous
In his Belfast flat, which Clendinning used as the office for his architectural practice, the main room of the Victorian attic was painted entirely in white. The furniture was of his own design and was upholstered in off-white tweed, while goatskin rugs covered the floor.

Below left
In the dining area of his London house, the glass-topped dining table and upholstered chairs were designed by Clendinning.

Below right
A bust of the Roman emperor and philosopher Marcus Aurelius stood in the green-painted conservatory.

Right
Mirrors were used throughout Clendinning's Belfast flat to give an illusion of space. Here, a corner of the flat was painted in bright red, in contrast to the all-white look that reigned in the rest of the interior.

Behind the brick façade of this nineteenth-century terrace in Canonbury, Max Clendinning's house was a startling study in minimalism. The entrance hall had crimson walls and a black-and-white tiled floor – off it lay the all-white sitting room that was furnished with Clendinning's cube-like modular furniture. White lino floor tiles blended into the white walls: the only non-white thing in the room was a wall motif in eau-de-nil. When Clendinning redecorated the room, he decided that the existing linen curtains looked too old-fashioned, so replaced them with polythene.

It was not just the sitting room that made a statement. The stairwell was covered in silver foil, with a mouse-grey carpet for the stair runner and the ceiling painted in a textured, greyish tone. Clendinning's office on the first floor was decorated in mustard, mauve and viridian, while the nearby bathroom was covered in murals by Clendinning's partner, the set designer Ralph Adron – psychedelic flourishes included camouflaging the wall heater so that it became the body of a large painted butterfly. In front of the bathroom light were four coloured discs, which revolved to bathe

the room in alternating shades of red, blue, green and purple.

On the top floor was an attic bedroom, with walls and ceiling completely covered in huge posters taken from billboards. The headboard, upholstered in brown felt, was criss-crossed by webbing holding postcards, notes and invitations. With William Morris curtains, an assortment of art-nouveau photograph frames, wooden cherubs and a pair of William De Morgan tiles propped against the wall, the overall effect was in complete contrast to the minimal white sitting room below.

SHIP-SHAPE

This Chelsea townhouse deftly mixed together pieces from different periods, resulting in an interior that still looks intriguing today. It is not surprising that the man behind it had a broad range of interests – from antiques to yacht design.

Above
At one end of the sitting room a set of painted wooden screens was used to cover the curtainless window. Paintings could be hung on the screen to add to the decorative effect.

Right
The view of the opposite end of the sitting room. Two large coffee tables demarcated the generous sitting area, while against the far wall was a desk used as an occasional study area.

Left above
A closer look at the wooden screens, this time in the dining area. The floor was covered in travertine tiles.

Left below
Another view of the dining room. The Louis XIV chairs were upholstered in floral-patterned linen that Bannenberg found in the United States. The side table, like the dining table, had a seventeenth-century oak top on a polished-steel base.

Below
In the bedroom, mirrored strips on the wall of cupboards played with the room's dimensions. The glass and painted wood table was designed by Bannenberg, while the gilded chair was one of a pair of Persian throne chairs.

Although this nineteenth-century house in Carlyle Square, Chelsea, was very much a family home, it doubled as a place of experimentation for the Australian-born designer and decorator Jon Bannenberg, who frequently changed the room settings and lighting to create different effects. His broad range of interests gave him a unique approach to design. In the early Fifties, he moved to London, where his interiors work across a variety of projects from exhibitions to house interiors grew out of his decorative arts business, Marble & Lemon, in Knightsbridge. However, he was best known for his work on yachts, taking on nearly 200 projects over his lifetime.

With yacht design, space was always at a premium, so interiors needed to be precisely planned and tended to incorporate the latest technology. A journalist visiting Bannenberg's house remarked that 'his lighting control system, covering spotlights, direct and indirect lighting, would scarcely be out of place in an experimental theatre'.

Natural light was also used to great effect. One of the most unusual decisions that Bannenberg made in the decoration of his own house was to completely eliminate curtains, despite living on a busy street in Chelsea. Throughout most of the day and night, the large windows of the house were left free from covering. For moments when privacy was deemed desirable, a series of perforated, white-painted timber screens could be pulled into position, casting patterned shadows across the rooms.

A white-and-orange colour palette dominated the spacious sitting room, which had a substantial sitting area demarcated by two large rectangular coffee tables.

Beyond it stood a grand piano, and beyond that a desk flanked by a pair of bookcases. Each area, whether for sitting, entertaining or working, was clearly defined. This intelligent use of space continued throughout the house. Although the kitchen and dining room were combined, each of the two areas had a very different feel. The kitchen area was colourful but highly functional, while the dining area was

lavishly decorated and designed as a space for entertaining. The main bedroom and bathroom were similarly conjoined – the bathroom was a large carpeted room with a freestanding bath and upholstered window seat, decorated in a similar manner to the bedroom. By questioning conventional layouts, Bannenberg achieved a house that was as well tailored as one of his yachts.

MUSIC & MAYHEM

CASE STUDY | SEPTEMBER 1968

Home to the composer Lionel Bart, this house off the Fulham Road in Chelsea became known for its owner's legendary parties. With its labyrinthine layout and unusual interiors, it was where everyone from The Beatles to The Rolling Stones came to let their hair down.

Left
Bart's bedroom overlooked the main living area. The electronically operated curtains were just one of the many up-to-the-minute conveniences that Bart had fitted throughout the house. In front of the television set was a BKF 'Butterfly' chair.

Above
This corner of the oak-panelled study retained the house's Edwardian feel, with leather chairs and a mahogany desk.

Below
The tiled kitchen was fitted out with the latest gadgets – most notably the huge fridge and oven.

Right
Cast-iron candelabra and a matching chandelier were made to Bart's design. Along with the elaborately pelmeted bay window, they created a theatrical effect in the vaulted, double-height living room.

St Dunstan's Priory on Seymour Road had been described by a previous tenant as 'an Edwardian monster'. Steeped in Arts and Crafts, the Priory needed significant remodelling when Lionel Bart bought it. However, the composer amped up the house's faux-historicism rather than toning it down. From the lavatory that resembled a gothic oak throne to the pair of huge, heavy iron candelabras in the vaulted-roofed drawing room, Bart meshed the style of the Sixties with an equally fashionable nostalgia for the past.

With 27 rooms, the house was large and rambling. At first-floor level was the enormous double-height drawing room, and overlooking this, at mezzanine level, was Bart's bedroom. In contrast to many of the other rooms, this room was extremely modern in appearance, from the shag-pile carpet to the curtains that could be closed at the touch of a button. The same gadgetry was to be found throughout the house: the drawing room boasted a remote-controlled screen that descended from the ceiling so that films could be projected upon it. Given the sheer number of clever decorative tricks and Bart's skills as a host, it is no surprise that this eccentric property was known as the 'Fun Palace'.

UNIVERSITY CHALLENGE

CASE STUDY | SEPTEMBER 1969

Built on the site of an old stable yard, this house was designed for the first principal of the recently founded Stirling University, creating a modern, minimally furnished space for both official entertaining and family living.

Right above
The house's modern exterior retained something of the look of the old stable yard, with concrete walls mimicking the appearance of a series of loose boxes.

Right below
Once through the front door, visitors entered a spacious entrance hall.

Far right
The dining room was situated at the south-west corner of the house. The living area was open-plan, so the sitting area was located behind the partition while the kitchen was to the right.

Below
The hallway acted as a gallery for the owners' collection of modern paintings.

Right
The L-shaped sitting area had two walls of windows, to make the most of the views of the Scottish countryside.

Far right
Although the kitchen was small, it represented an extremely efficient use of space, with a wall of built-in cupboards providing ample storage.

As the first principal of Stirling University, Tom Cottrell was given the freedom to design his own house for himself and his family. The university had been built largely from scratch on a greenfield site just outside the compact city, and its pleasant location meant that living on campus was an attractive option. A potential site caught his eye – an old stable yard that had belonged to an earlier house, set on a high rocky outcrop surrounded by trees and with views of a loch, and beyond that of Stirling Castle and the Wallace Memorial.

The university commissioned the architects Morris and Steedman to build the house. They used as much as possible of the old stone from the ruined stables in the new building, and built the house in an L-shape using two walls of the former courtyard. These two walls were unbroken by windows or doors – giving the house increased privacy on those two sides. By contrast, the other sides had large floor-to-ceiling windows that made the most of the sun and the spectacular views. The hall, living room and dining area were given additional height by raising the roof, to create an impressive space for official entertaining.

Throughout the house, the rooms were painted white and minimally furnished. Recessed ceiling lights and spotlights provided discreet lighting, and added to the slick, modern feel of the building. Because of its unusual design, a wide, angular hallway ran the length of the house, and this was used to display Cottrell's personal collection of art. The university's new principal was a keen collector and had bought a number of modern pieces over the years; this interest in modern art has subsequently become a feature of Stirling University itself, as over the years it has consistently invested in work by Scottish artists to enliven its campus.

3. DECORATION

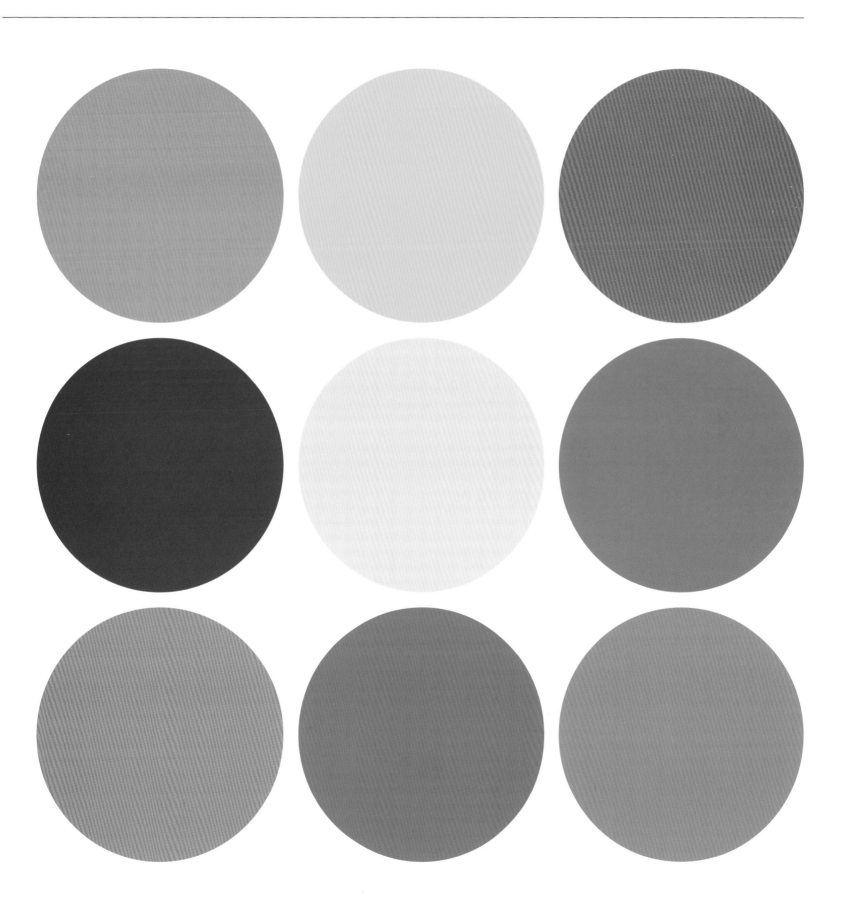

PRINCIPLES TO GOVERN DECORATION
MADE TO PLAN

Throughout the Sixties, House & Garden *collaborated with companies, property developers and television programmes to create up-to-the-minute room schemes. Although set designs, no matter how carefully constructed, were never going to achieve quite the same effect as a lived-in interior, they do present a fascinating insight into the principles that governed the decoration of domestic interiors in the Sixties. Because these were designed to appeal to the mass market, they represent the median of Sixties interior decoration rather than the pinnacle. While in Part 2 we looked at how the decade's leading taste-makers decorated their homes, the sets shown here represent the style of decoration that appealed to popular taste, designed to be both long-lasting and practical.*

Left
A 1967 bedroom designed for the International Wool Secretariat to show off wool products. This vibrant scheme had walls and curtains in a 'Venus' wool weave from Tamesa Fabrics, teamed with a ginger wool carpet, a Victorian bentwood chair and chests of drawers from Liberty.

Above
The main bedroom of a 1967 room set designed for a BBC programme called *In Your Place.* Built-in units were covered with the same paper that was used on the walls – a pink, green and white 'Rozel' pattern from Sanderson. The upholstered chair was by Gomme.

Previous
A 1964 scheme designed by *House & Garden* for Harrods, this cottage living room had Magistretti rush-seated chairs and Formica-fronted kitchen units from Wrighton. Above the units, a colourful 'Cafe Concert' wallpaper from Cole & Son competed for attention with a pair of Mexican pottery cats.

Left
This 1967 room set had a youthful feel – an assortment of pop posters was teamed with fabrics in red, black and white. The sofa was covered in a wool fabric from Tibor while the lacquered coffee table was from Liberty.

Below
Another 1964 set for Harrods shows a scheme for a town flat – this room doubled as both entrance hall and study. The tiles around the fireplace were designed by Alan Wallwork of Greenwich Studios. The furniture was from Artek and the tableware from Rosenthal.

Previous
Block colours abound in this 1967 set showing a sitting room-cum-study area. The desk and chair were designed by Robert Heritage, while the sofa and coffee table were made by Impetus.

Below
The clue to the sponsor behind the interiors of this 1968 show house lies in the ram-motif wall panels. Taken from a Renaissance fresco by Francesco del Cossa, they nodded to the fact that nearly everything in this sitting room was made of wool, including the wallcoverings – part of a promotion by the International Wool Secretariat to showcase the possibilities of this natural material. Another view of this room is shown overleaf.

Right
Flock wallpaper from Cole & Son, gold silk bedcovers and an assortment of antiques borrowed from Portobello Road dealers created a sumptuous effect in this bedroom set from 1964.

MODERN HOUSES
AND CONVERSIONS

BOLD, MODERN DESIGNS
FURNITURE

The Fifties had seen a revolution in furniture design. Gone was the fashion for reproduction furniture that had lingered long into the early decades of the century, as the modern designs that had originated in the Thirties finally found widespread popularity. In the United States, Charles and Ray Eames had led the way in popularizing this new style of furniture in metal and wood, and companies such as Knoll manufactured furniture by leading international designers. The Scandinavian influence had left a lasting international impression and had helped to popularize the use of teak and rosewood, resulting in the lighter-coloured furniture of the mid-century period. Britain had its own crop of designers producing innovative furniture, such as Robin Day, who created numerous pieces for Hille, and Ernest Race, who was commissioned to furnish the British Pavilion at the World's Fair in Brussels in 1958.

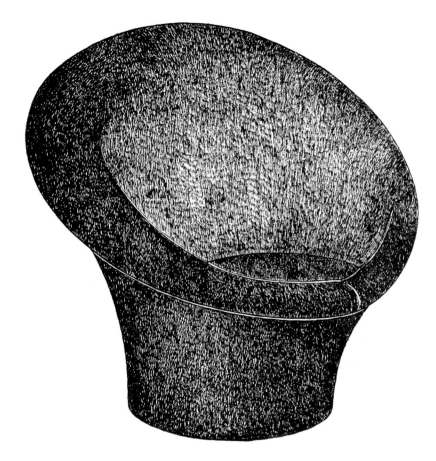

Left
Plastic finds its way into virtually every component of this 1968 room. Square windows are covered in coloured plastic sheets. Cube-like armchairs are covered in pink vinyl, and moulded plastic chairs by Robin Day for Hille stand behind them. A Japanese gold plastic garland – then a novelty – is suspended from the ceiling as a final flourish.

Above
This 'Mushroom' chair by French interior designer Pierre Paulin appeared in 1960. Manufactured by Artifort, it heralded the curved forms that would become synonymous with Sixties design.

Below
Below are two chairs that Finmar
introduced to the UK in 1960: a Danish
'Ditzel' armchair, by Nanna and Jørgen
Ditzel (left), and Arne Jacobsen's 'Swan'
armchair (right). Beneath it are three
views of the 'Cone' chair by Verner
Panton. Like Jacobsen's 'Swan', this
Danish design is from 1958, but was first
imported into the UK in 1960 by Heal's.

At the start of the Sixties, the aesthetic was beginning to change. The slim, modernist designs that dominated Fifties furniture were being replaced by more functional, rectilinear styles. The Scandinavian school of design had become ubiquitous by the early Sixties, and teak was the dominant material used for this type of furniture. Scandinavian, and particularly Danish, furniture was imported into Britain and sold by companies such as Scandia and Finmar. Imported furniture was expensive, and British manufacturers began to produce their own take on these designs.

One of the best known of these was E Gomme Ltd, manufacturers of the very popular G-Plan range, which had first appeared in 1952. In the early Sixties, the company commissioned Danish designer Ib Kofod-Larsen to create a bespoke range for them in teak and rosewood; this bore the stamp 'G-Plan Danish Design' and incorporated Kofod-Larsen's signature for added authenticity. The range sold well, and the collaboration continued throughout the decade. G-Plan wasn't the only British company to adopt this style: others included Nathan, Meredew, Younger and McIntosh. John and Sylvia Reid continued to design for the Nottingham-based company Stag in the Sixties, producing teak-and-metal dining room furniture that was perhaps inspired more by American than by Scandinavian design. That said, one of their bestselling styles was extremely revivalist: their 1964 'Minstrel' range was inspired by the eighteenth century. Ercol was another popular British company making furniture that was rooted in traditional English country styles, but still looked modern.

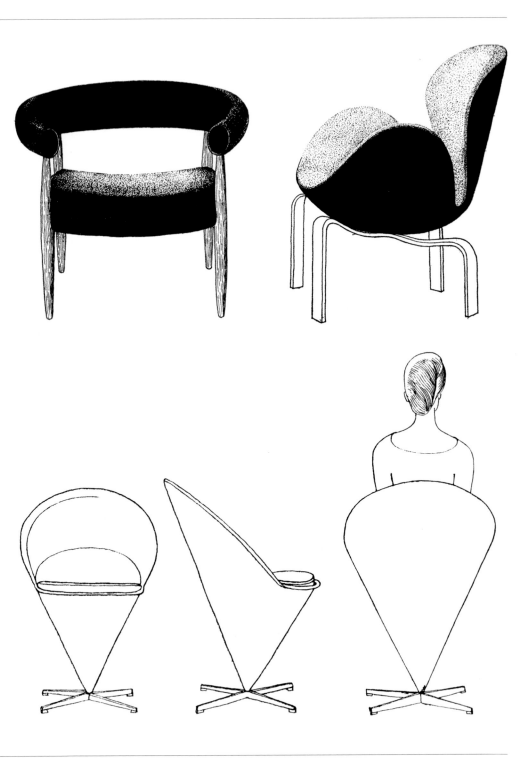

Below
A range of furniture that was available in 1966, with prices ranging from cheap to expensive.

Top row:
Polypropylene stacking chair by Robin Day; Windsor chair by Ercol; Heal's bentwood chair; Goods & Chattels bentwood chair; 'Dina Chair' by Ronald Carter; 'Stork' pedestal chair by Peter Dickinson for Race.

Second row:
Deck chair from Woolworth's; cane chair from Lord Roberts Memorial Workshops; canvas chair by Verner Panton; easy chair by Pete Withers; chair by Nicholas Frewing for Race; 'Queensdown' chair by Parker-Knoll.

Third row:
Kewlox folding table; pine table by Conran; gateleg G-Plan table by Gomme; extending table by Conran from Habitat.

Fourth row:
Sofabed by Vono; sofa bed by Buckingham Bedding specialists; G-Plan sofa bed by Gomme; sofa bed by G Fejer and E Pamphilon for Guy Rogers.

Fifth row:
Meredew's 'Simplifold' wall storage system; cupboard from Albany Mill; imported 'Norpine' shelves; six-drawer chest from F Austin; 'Opus 22' wardrobe by Walter Muller for Stag; cupboard by P & D Goble for Gimson & Slater .

As in the Fifties, Heal's was a leading retailer of good-quality modern furniture in the UK, both with its in-house designs and also with its imported furniture by Scandinavian, Italian and American designers. As pop culture seeped into design, plastic furniture became ever more popular, as it could be moulded into virtually any shape. Robin Day's polypropylene stacking chairs – seen in offices and universities across the world – were launched in 1963 and proved immensely successful, with millions sold. In 1962, Hille also began to produce Charles Eames designs under licence, including his iconic 'Lounge Chair (670)' and 'Ottoman (671)'. These were highly influential pieces of furniture that heralded a new direction in Sixties design, with sturdier, masculine forms, curving shapes and deep upholstery.

By the mid-Sixties, the vogue for Scandinavian furniture was starting to calm, and an interest in the new styles of furniture being produced by a younger generation of designers had sprung up instead. Race Furniture produced a range of affordably priced, white-painted plywood furniture by the young Northern Irish designer Max Clendinning. Another design that was much talked about was Peter Murdoch's polka-dot-patterned cardboard chairs, which were bought flat-packed and had a lifespan of just a couple of months. In 1966, Bernard Holdaway created (for Hull Traders) a range of brightly painted cylindrical chairs and tables made of compressed paper.

Although the lifespan of these paper creations was short, the plastic furniture from this period has lasted well. Popular designs included the 'Universale' chair

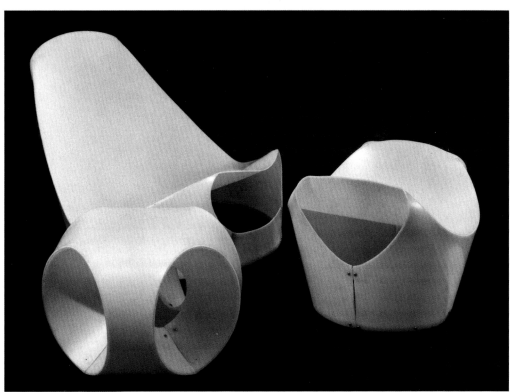

Below
Furniture took on a playful note in the Sixties – this fibreglass chair by Thornton & Sandberg, pictured in 1966, could be upholstered in a selection of bright colours and was sold at Heal's.

Right
A 1968 vinyl wallcovering from Crown is teamed with Lurashell's fibreglass chairs, which were described as having 'that space-age look'.

by Joe Colombo and the 'Selene' chair by Vico Magistretti. But probably the most in-your-face example of Sixties furniture was the Finnish designer Eero Aarnio's 'Ball Chair'. Made famous by its appearances in the television series *The Prisoner* (1967–8) and in the film *The Italian Job* (1969), it was nevertheless fated not to become a household staple. Partly this was due to its high price point, but it was also down to the fact that it was too large to fit through most door frames.

By the late Sixties, the resurgence of interest in antique styles meant that many decorators preferred to work with antique furniture – using an eclectic range of styles that ranged from Thirties Art Deco to brown furniture that typically dated from Georgian to Victorian. Younger designers who were furnishing their first studios or flats made use of modular furniture produced by companies such as Habitat. Inflatable furniture, though hardly a long-term investment, held a novelty value and could be assembled and packed away at will, and was in keeping with the transitory, nomadic attitude displayed by many of the young taste-makers of Swinging London.

Left
Curtains in 'Impact' by Evelyn Brooks and a seventeenth-century portrait of Sir Thomas Wentworth contrast with a desk and chair from Greaves & Thomas in 1966. The black upholstered 'Leo' chairs were by Robin Day for Hille.

Below
When these two new chairs were shown in the August 1960 issue of *House & Garden*, neither model was available in Britain. On the left was the 'Large Eve' armchair by Kerstin Hörlin-Holmquist, manufactured by the Swedish company Triva. On the right was a moulded plastic chair by George Nelson.

Bottom left
The furniture for this 1966 studio scheme can be spotted on page 187. The hammock was imported by Danasco and sold at Habitat.

Bottom right
A 1962 glass-and-aluminium coffee table by Roger Brockbank of Design Associates.

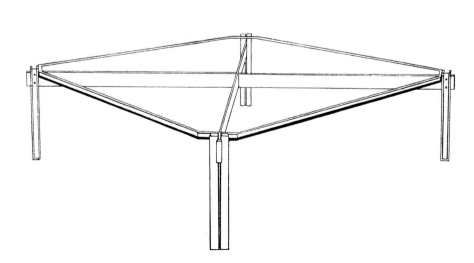

The following four pages showcase the influx of new furniture that was newly available in the UK in 1962: a mix of Scandinavian imports and British designs.

Below
The large chair is teak and leather, from Danasco. *Top row, from left:* 'Carolina' armchair, by Greaves & Thomas; 'Formstol' stacking chair, by Frederick Restall; 'DC1' dining chair, by G Hoffstead for Uniflex; dining chair by E Ihnatovitch for W J Mars; Swedish dining chair, by Rix for Heal's Continental Range.

Bottom row, clockwise from left: 'Duet' chair, by John and Sylvia Reid for Stag; Danish chair, imported by Danasco; 'Multalum' settee, by George Kasparian; the end of a 'Pendennis' dining table, by Robert Heritage, made by Archie Shine for Heal's; Danish dining table, by Bent Anderson, imported by Scandia.

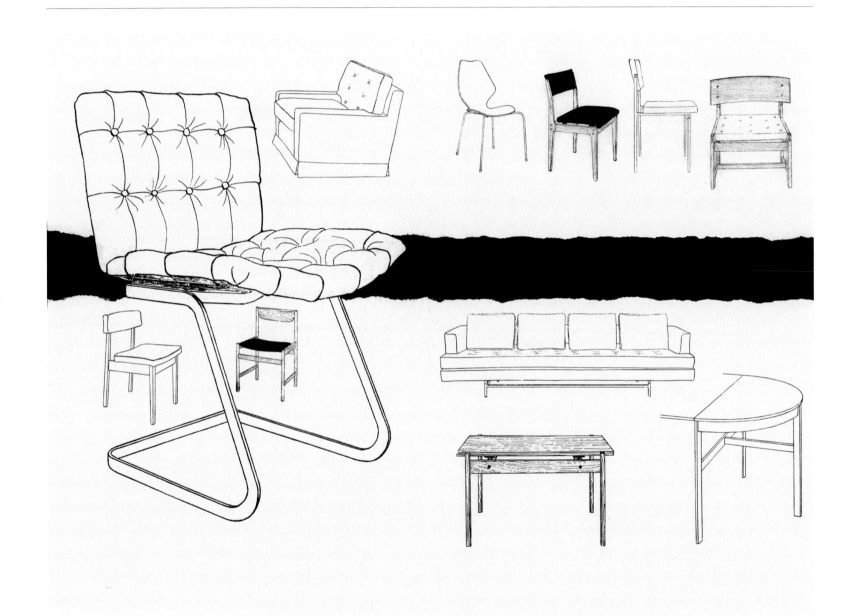

Deep-buttoning revived for new comfort

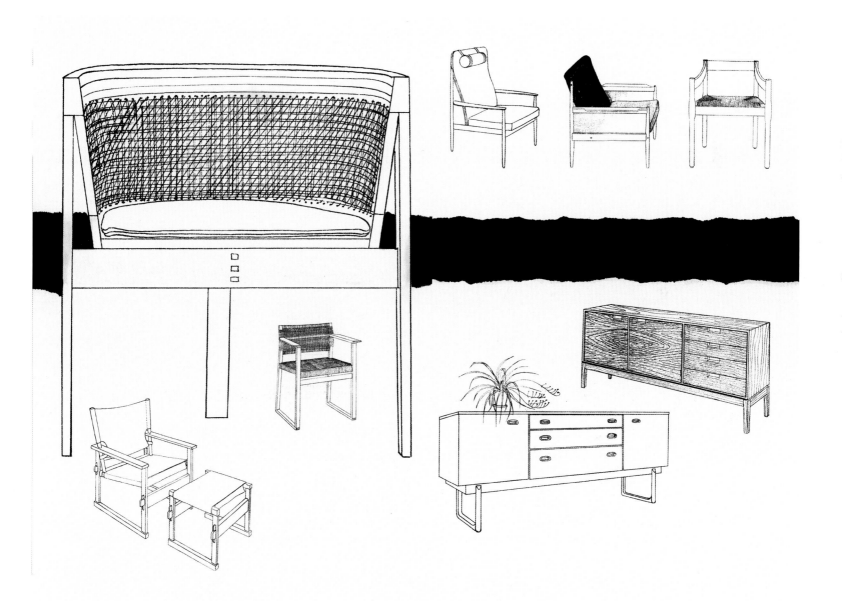

At last—bold angles <u>and</u> curves

Construction details are unashamedly shown

Below

Top row, from left:
'8022' trolley, by Ib Kofod-Larsen for
G-Plan; chest of drawers and dressing
table, by Erik Worts, imported by
Bergdala; 'Erith' chest of drawers,
by Richard Forwood; 'Big' chair, by
Jørgen Pedersen.

Bottom row, from left:
Coffee table, by William Plunkett of
A & R Duckworth Associates; 'GF40/4'
stacking chair, by David Rolland; circular
side table, by William Plunkett; stackable
table, by Magistretti.

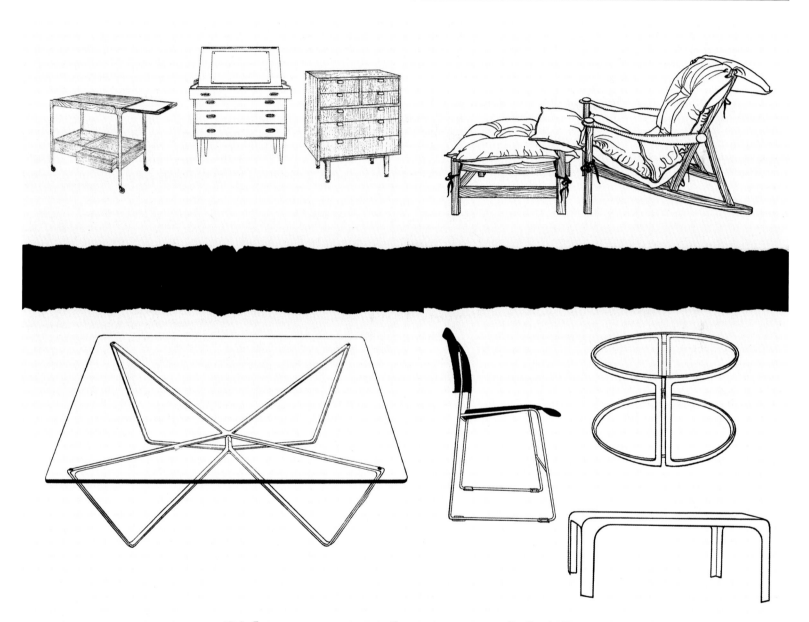

Rich textures complement smooth finishes

Below
This foam-filled four-seater 'Crown Settee', designed by Flemming Ager, won a competition sponsored by United Foam that was held in 1968. It was sold through Oscar Woollens, a furniture shop on Finchley Road.

'INNOVATIONS IN INTERIOR DESIGN'

AUGUST 1966

An article published in House & Garden *in January 1967 looked at the latest developments in furniture and speculated on how furniture might evolve in the future.*

'Much of our new furniture is being designed in many standardised small components, assembled to serve a variety of needs, simply because standardised units are cheap and easy to manufacture. And the current desire to make a piece of furniture out of a single sheet of ply or aluminum or in one complete process is not merely an exquisite mathematical exercise but much more a question of economics – pure and simple.

'Paradoxically, as our standards of living rise our standard of living space diminishes, and this sad fact also helps to account for designers' preoccupation with knock-down constructions, stackable, inflatable and foldaway frames, and their quest for degrees of flexibility and mobility. In simple terms, flexible furniture is designed to do several jobs. Mobility, at its most primitive, is furniture on castors, and the castor is certainly on its way back.

'Theoretically, mobility makes possible a more fluid employment of that volume which the innocent and uninitiated still fondly call the house. The notion of snail-like humans, carrying their inflatable carapace on their backs, may sound pretty far fetched, but it has its roots in indestructible arguments. We have population out-stripping accommodation in one half of the world, and in the other half an increasing pattern for one family occupying two houses (one urban the other rural). Hence the idea of inflatable mobile package structures. Such theories have far-reaching effects on design students. Suddenly it seems, at least one design student in every art school in the country is working on an inflatable project or "capsule".

'The fashion for capsule living has yet to take off, but the transition from the very restrained Scandinavian modern style that was in fashion at the beginning of the Sixties to the fantastical productions made of plastic that dominated late-Sixties design made this decade one of the most interesting for experimentation and innovation in furniture design.'

Below left
By 1966 most British design lovers were familiar with Danish and Swedish furniture – however, Finnish designs were also becoming increasingly sought after, such as these pieces from Haimi of Finland.

Below
This collection of futuristic plastic seating, available in 1969, was by the Italian designer Mario Sabot.

Bottom
Component parts of a Norwegian chair by Sven Ivar Dysthe flank the finished item in 1964. In the UK, these chairs were imported by Westnofa.

INNOVATION & TRADITION
MATERIALS

Although the Sixties may be best remembered for their use of plastic, more traditional materials such as glass, ceramics and textiles – both natural and synthetic – also reflected the aesthetic of the decade.

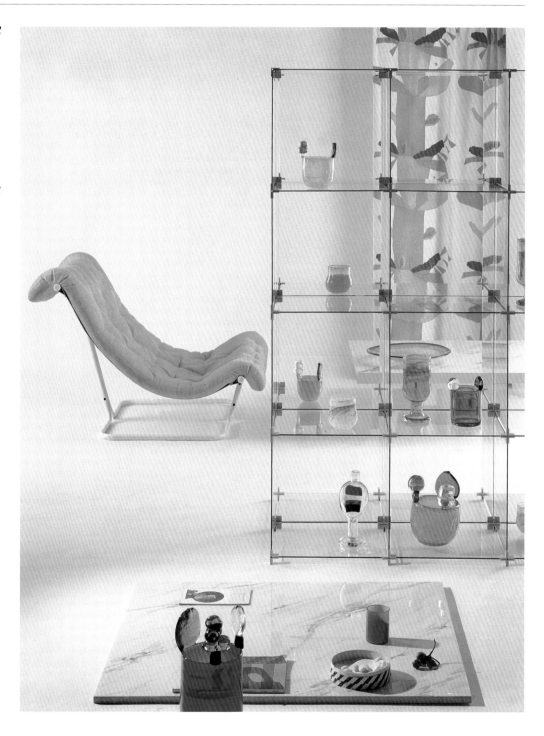

Left
Bright motifs and lots of plastics abound in this 1968 scheme. In the foreground is a Max Clendinning armchair with a matching side table (with the stylist's addition of a mass of plastic piping snaking out of it). The yellow-and-white chest of drawers was by David Goodship for Meredew, the wall-covering was from David Whitehead, while the table and sideboard were from Uniflex.

Right
Scandinavian glass was popular throughout the Sixties: this 1969 collection of glass objects and vases was by Oiva Toikka at the Notsjö factory in Finland.

TEXTILES

During the Fifties, Britain was internationally recognized for its innovative and lively textiles. Designers such as Lucienne Day, Marian Mahler and Jacqueline Groag pioneered bright, hand-drawn motifs that used organic shapes and scientific forms for inspiration. Companies such as Edinburgh Weavers, David Whitehead, Heal's and Liberty were also vital in commissioning designers, both freelance and in-house, to come up with cutting-edge new patterns. By the Sixties, these designs were becoming simpler and more linear, with more emphasis placed on the texture of the fabrics, as coarsely woven textiles became popular. The colour palette had also changed, taking its cue from nature, with browns, greens and pale blues predominating. Many designs were commissioned from leading artists, such as Sanderson's 'Stones of Bath' fabric, designed by British artist John Piper and appearing on

Left
A 1964 collection of new fabrics, all winners of that year's Cotton Board Awards, created by a mix of established and emerging textile designers. *Top row:* 'Pheonix', by Joyce Mattock; 'Stanhope', by Howard Carter. *Second row:* 'My Love', by Natalie Gibson; 'Concord', by Grace Selvanayagam; 'Gilliflower', by Gillian Farr. *Third row:* 'Abberley', by Ann Sutton; 'CP5014', by Barbara Payze; 'Eclipse', by Anna Potworowska. *Bottom row:* 'Butterfly', by Margaret Bonito; 'Colourscope', by Sheila Yale; 'Cockade', by Joan McFetrich.

Right
A selection of Conran fabrics from Habitat create a colourful atmosphere in 1967. Gillian Farr's 'Gilliflower' from the previous picture was still in fashion and can be spotted on a cushion.

Below
An assortment of bed linen, towels, bathmats and tea towels from 1967. The boy-and-lion hand towel was from Fieldcrest. The Swedish mushroom-print linen tea towel was by Almedahls. The wine-bottle tea towel was by Robinson & Cleaver, and the 'Periwinkle' tea towel to the right of it was a pattern by Lucienne Day.

Right
Furniture makers were increasingly offering bright patterns as part of their in-house fabric selections, as can be seen with this sofa from Hampstead-based company Interiors in 1966. The curtain and matching wallpaper by Warners were inspired by a Renaissance pattern, while the lampshade is in a Liberty print called 'Henrietta'.

the market in 1962. This pattern had a large-scale repeat, a style that became increasingly common as the decade progressed. These worked well when the fabrics were used in large quantities, such as for the floor-to-ceiling curtains that screened the French windows that were becoming ever more popular architectural elements in urban and rural houses alike. Large-scale repeats of floral patterns gave rise to the 'flower power' look so typical of Sixties decoration, and which sold well, especially from the mid-Sixties onwards. The motifs were often extremely simplified and stylized, in bold colours, and were aimed at the youthful end of the market – these designs were an early staple of Habitat's textile range. The Finnish company Marimekko also produced designs in this style. Op art also found its way into textile design, with Victor Vasarely being commissioned to create designs for Edinburgh Weavers, while Barbara Brown's designs for Heal's often employed strongly geometric motifs. At Hull Traders, Shirley Craven also produced a number of abstract designs that tapped into this trend.

As the forward-looking, modernist aesthetic that dominated the start of the Sixties gave way to a renewed interest in past styles, old editions of Victorian and Regency designs were reissued, sometimes in different colourways, while the Art Nouveau and Art Deco revivals also had an impact on textiles, with a proliferation of swirling, richly coloured patterns. An Eastern influence also appeared in textile design, and complex patterns, in both large- and small-scale repeats, were used to create a strong decorative statement, often with wallpaper and textiles in the same motif.

CERAMICS

Hand-made stoneware became particularly sought-after in Britain in the mid-twentieth century, and there was a proliferation of small potteries inspired by the work of Bernard Leach. His 1940 text, *A Potter's Book*, set out an aesthetic for studio pottery that was based around pre-industrial Asian and English ceramics. The Leach Pottery in St Ives produced a range of Standard Ware in the Forties that attracted a lot of attention amid the wartime restrictions. Towards the end of the Fifties, factories began to mimic the look of the robust brown stoneware produced by small-scale potteries. This ceramics style was fostered by the demand for oven-to-tableware, which suited the Mediterranean recipes that were spreading to Britain – and also had the advantage of minimizing washing up.

Left
An assortment of Venini glass enlivens this 1965 selection of household accessories, notably the striped tumblers and the orange striped bottle that stands under the small table. On the floor to the left, is a rectangular glass bottle (also in orange, though you can't tell from the photograph) from Rosenthal; the remainder of the pottery and glassware on the floor was sourced from the Army & Navy Stores.

Right above
Synthetic tableware emerged as a competitor to ceramics. This 1962 table displays Plexiglas bowls from Danasco and melamine cups, saucers and side plates from Finnish Designs.

Right below
A collection of egg cups made from a single piece of moulded plastic, designed by Robert Thurtle in 1964.

Below left
An assortment of coloured tiles from 1967, some imported, others manufactured in the UK, illustrates the trend for using rustic tiles to decorate bathrooms or kitchen splashbacks.

Below right
This black basalt vase with a gold rim, pictured in 1967, was designed by Peter Wall for Wedgwood.

Bottom right
A tumbler by Notsjö, alongside two vacuum jugs and a cup and saucer. Pictured in 1963, all pieces were Finnish and imported by Danasco.

The textural qualities that were appearing in textile design during the Sixties also found their way into ceramics. Muted colours and roughly textured surfaces were in vogue, and factories produced ceramics with relief-printed designs.

Midwinter was one of the most foremost British makers of tableware throughout the Fifties and early Sixties. Its abstract patterns such as 'Sienna' (1962) and 'Mexicana' (1966) were all popular with consumers. As the Sixties progressed, Midwinter patterns became reliant on stylized floral and Eastern motifs, which although trend-driven were commercial failures, and the company was taken over by a competitor, J & G Meakin, in 1968. Two other British companies that were still going strong at the end of the Sixties were Hornsea and Portmeirion.

Hornsea Pottery was established in the 1949 and its innovative designs, typically with impressed linear or geometric motifs, proved popular throughout the Sixties. Its early ceramics were glazed with a matt white base colour, but as the decade progressed earthier colours such as browns and greens were common. Denby's 'Arabesque' pattern utilized a similar colour scheme and was another bestselling range. Portmeirion produced very textural designs such as the 'Totem' range of 1963; other notable patterns included the abstract 'Variations' range (1963) and the exotically patterned 'Magic City' (1966). While studio potteries offered a counterculture alternative to mass-produced factory designs, the increasingly primitive, abstract patterns and the popularity of stoneware were trends that could be found in both factory production line and potter's studio.

Below left
Screen-printed tiles from Pilkington-
Carter cover all four walls of this
bathroom from 1967.

Below right
Three tables from 1969, covered in
brightly patterned tiles. *From top:*
'Cameo 15' by H & R Johnson; Spanish
tiles from Casa Pupo; and matt-glazed
ceramic tiles from Polycell.

GLASS

Throughout the Sixties, the art glass market was dominated by Italian and Scandinavian companies. In Italy, the hand-blown glass produced on the Venetian island of Murano was notable for its bright colours and elongated forms, often embellished with decorative details. In Britain, companies such as Heal's, Harrods and Liberty stocked designs from leading Italian glass producers such as Venini, Seguso and Barovier & Toso.

In contrast to the bright flamboyance of Italian designs, Scandinavian glass was characterized by its cool tones and restrained shapes. Leading companies – Kosta and Orrefors in Sweden, Iittala in Finland, and Holmegaard in Denmark – exported their glass internationally. In the Sixties, the organic forms of the previous decade were being superseded by more precise, geometric shapes. From the mid-Sixties, Scandinavian glass began to display a more textural element, often achieved by blowing glass into roughly hewn wooden moulds to produce uneven tactile surfaces – Timo Sarpaneva's bark and ice textured vases and range of 'Festivo' candlesticks are examples of this technique.

A similar use of texture, although teamed with much brighter colours, was used by the long-established British company Whitefriars in the mid-Sixties, with its range of vases designed by Geoffrey Baxter. Baxter used bark, brick and nails in his moulds to achieve a variety of effects, and the range sold extremely well. Other British glass companies still relied on traditional cut-glass designs, hence the appreciation for Italian and Scandinavian glassware among aficionados of modern design.

Left
A ship's decanter and a tumbler – both Finnish, made by Karhula-Iittala and imported to Britain by Danasco. Pictured in 1967.

Below
Top row from left:
This 1965 image shows 'Manhattan' jug and glass, by Riedel; Swedish beer tankard, from Portmeirion; tall opaque blue glass, from Liberty; cut-glass tumbler, by Royal Tudor; tumblers (large and small) and champagne glass, from Liberty; green glass, from Army & Navy.

Middle row from left:
'Mambo' glass and tumbler, from Designs of Scandinavia; vase, by Boda; decanter and set of three glasses, by Orrefors; pair of opaque-glass vases, by Magnor; tankard and set of tumblers, by Bergdala; pair of Norwegian glass vases, by Magnor; decanter, by Orrefors.

Bottom row from left:
Glass and decanter, by Riedel; glass, by Edinburgh Crystal; Italian highball glass, from Woolands; champagne glass, by Sarnen; decanter, by Edinburgh Crystal; sherry glass and goblet, by Portmeirion; decanter, by Boda.

METALWARE

Contemporary metalware reflected the Scandinavian modern look, which had earlier been honed by designers such as Georg Jensen. A new crop of British designers was responsible for creating some of the decade's most enduring designs: David Mellor, Robert Welch and Gerald Benney, all contemporaries at the Royal College of Art, were at the forefront of British metalware. Mellor, from Sheffield, famous for its steel industries, designed popular ranges of stainless steel cutlery. 'Symbol' in 1962 had an eight-piece setting instead of the more traditional 11 pieces, while his 1967 'Thrift' set, for canteens, hospitals and prisons, had only five. Mellor and Welch both combined silversmithing with industrial design. Welch's 'Alvaston' tableware range for Old Hall was the company's main seller during the Sixties, and the stainless steel tea sets were particularly sought after. Benney, meanwhile, experimented with new techniques, including hammering silver for a bark-like effect (much copied during the Sixties). Towards the end of the decade he developed an interest in enamelling metal, and enlisted a Norwegian master craftsman to train his staff. From new shapes to adventurous finishes, these designers injected new life into British metalware.

Left
Robert Heritage for Yote 1964 stainless steel cutlery with polycarbonate handles.

Above right
An 'Embassy' teapot by David Mellor in 1964; it was originally designed for British embassies around the world.

Right
Stainless steel salad servers in 1967, designed by G Bellamy for George Wostenholm & Son.

Below left
A stainless steel tea set designed by David Mellor and pictured in 1967.

Below right
David Mellor's seven-piece 'Triad' setting, for Walker & Hall, pictured in 1965.

Bottom left
Robert Welch designed the stainless steel sauce boat, shown here in 1967, while the silver carving knife and fork were by Robin Beresford.

Bottom right
A 1963 collection of Scandinavian tableware. The imported designs influenced a new generation of British metalware designers.

Below
More Scandinavian metalware in 1963.
Top row, from left: copper pans, imported
by Svensk; Danish stainless steel frying
pan with teak handle, imported by James
Howarth; Finnish pottery jar, by Arabia,
from Danasco; cutlery by Skandia.
Bottom row, from left: 'Spectra' stainless
steel cutlery, by Skandia; Norwegian
stainless steel and teak pan,
imported by Condrup; Norwegian
ivory-handled carvers, imported by
James Howarth.

BIBLIOGRAPHY & STOCKISTS

Bony, Anne (2004) *Furniture and Interiors of the 1960s*, Thames & Hudson

Bradbury, Dominic (2014) *Mid-Century Modern Complete*, Thames & Hudson

Casey, Andrew (2014) *Lucienne Day*, ACC

Crow, Thomas (2014) *The Long March of Pop: Art, Music and Design, 1930-1995*, Yale University Press

Evans, Paul (2010) *The 1960s Home*, Shire Publishing

Fiell, Charlotte and Peter (2000) *60s Decorative Art*, Taschen

Fiell, Charlotte and Peter (2013) *Scandinavian Design*, Taschen

Fiell, Charlotte and Peter (2015) *Robert Welch: Design, Craft and Industry*, Laurence King

Goodden, Joanna (1984) *At the Sign of the Fourposter: A History of Heal's*, Heal & Son

Harling, Robert (1964) *House & Garden: The Modern Interior*, Condé Nast

Heathcote, David (2004) *Sixtiestyle: Home Decoration and Furnishings from the 1960s*, Middlesex University Press

Jackson, Lesley (2011) *20th Century Pattern Design: Textile and Wallpaper Pioneers*, Mitchell Beazley

Jackson, Lesley (2000) *20th Century Factory Glass*, Rizzoli

Jackson, Lesley (2000) *The Sixties: Decade of Design Revolution*, Phaidon

Leach, Bernard (1940) *A Potter's Book*, Faber

Lutyens, Dominic (2013) *Living with Mid-century Collectibles*, Ryland Peters & Small

Miller, Judith (2012) *Mid-century Modern: Living with Mid-century Modern Design*, Miller's

Quinn, Bradley (2004) *Mid-century Modern: Interiors, Furniture, Design, Details*, Conran Octopus

Rice, Paul (2002) *British Studio Ceramics*, The Crowood Press

Many of the companies featured in this book are still going strong, while many of the furniture designs remain in production by companies licensed to manufacture them to the original specifications. Where possible, their websites are listed below.

Alessi www.alessi.com
Anglepoise www.anglepoise.com
Biba www.mybiba.com
Cole & Son www.cole-and-son.com
The Conran Shop www.conranshop.co.uk
Edinburgh Weavers www.edinburghweavers.com
Ercol www.ercol.co.uk
Fornasetti www.fornasetti.com
G P & J Baker www.gpandbaker.com
G Plan www.gplan.co.uk
Habitat www.habitat.co.uk
Harrods www.harrods.com
Heal's www.heals.co.uk
Hille www.hille.co.uk
Iittala www.iittala.com
John Lewis www.johnlewis.com
Kartell www.kartell.com
Knoll www.knoll.com
The Leach Pottery www.leachpottery.com
Liberty www.liberty.co.uk
Marimekko www.marimekko.com
Portmeirion www.portmeirion.co.uk
Race Furniture www.racefurniture.com
Sanderson www.sanderson-uk.com
Venini www.venini.com
Vitra www.vitra.com

PICTURE CREDITS

Page 1: August 1960
Pages 2 and 3: March 1967
Page 4: September 1968

All photographs © The Condé Nast
Publications Ltd

Photographers:

Anthony Denney, Robert Freson, Martin
Harrison, Ruan O'Lochlain, James
Mortimer, Ugo Mulas, Peter Rand, Cyril
Readjones, John Vaughan, Michael
Wickham, Caradog Williams and John
Wingrove

Illustrators:

Rosemary Grimble and Martin Simmons

INDEX

INDEX

An Hachette UK Company
www.hachette.co.uk

First published in Great Britain in 2016
by Conran Octopus,
a division of Octopus Publishing Group Ltd
Carmelite House
50 Victoria Embankment
London
EC4Y 0DZ
www.octopusbooks.co.uk

Distributed in the US by
Hachette Book Group
1290 Avenue of the Americas
4th and 5th Floors
New York, NY 10020

Distributed in Canada by
Canadian Manda Group
664 Annette St.
Toronto, Ontario, Canada M6S 2C8

ISBN 978 1 84091 664 5

A CIP catalogue record for this book is
available from the British Library

Printed and bound in China

10 9 8 7 6 5 4 3 2 1

Every effort has been made to reproduce
the colours in this book accurately; however,
the printing process can lead to some
discrepancies. The colour samples provided
should be used as a guideline only.

Publisher Alison Starling
Editor Pauline Bache
Creative Director Jonathan Christie
Assistant Production Manager
Caroline Alberti

Special thanks to:
Harriet Wilson, Brett Croft, Ben Evans,
Ulrika Becker, Frith Carlisle, Poppy Roy
and Hatta Byng at The Condé Nast
Publications Ltd.

April

House & Garden

THREE SHILLINGS

e Many Moods of Modern

sentation flower print Rhododendron

TYARD HOUSE NEAR GAINSBOROUGH

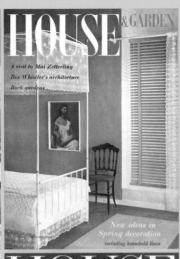

HOUSE **& GARDEN**

A visit to Mai Zetterling
Rex Whistler's architecture
Rock gardens

New ideas in
Spring decoration
including household linen

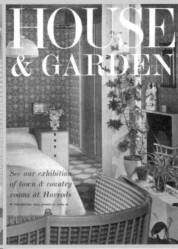

HOUSE & GARDEN

*See our exhibition
of town & country
rooms at Harrods*

IN THE CENTRAL HALL (MARCH 14—APRIL 15)

HOUSE & GARDEN

APRIL 1967 FOUR SHILLINGS

THE ROOMS
WHERE
THE FORSYTES
LIVED

HOW TO USE
TILES IN
YOUR HOME

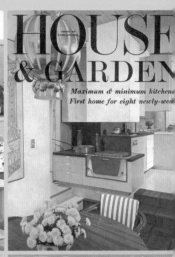

HOUSE & GARDEN

JANUARY 1967 THREE SHILLINGS

*Maximum & minimum kitchens
First home for eight newly-weds*

HOUSE **& GARDEN**

My favourite room

BY VANESSA REDGRAVE
BARBARA GOALEN, WOLF MANKOWITZ
VALERIE HOBSON
LÆLIA DUCHESS OF WESTMINSTER
AND OTHERS IN THE NEWS

JANUARY THREE SHILLINGS

HOUSE & GARDEN

JANUARY THREE SHILLINGS

All about Entertaining

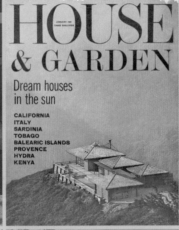

HOUSE & GARDEN

JANUARY 1961 THREE SHILLINGS

Dream houses
in the sun

CALIFORNIA
ITALY
SARDINIA
TOBAGO
BALEARIC ISLANDS
PROVENCE
HYDRA
KENYA

HOUSE & GARDEN

JANUARY 1961 THREE SHILLINGS

Houses of fantasy and escape

HOUSE & GARDEN

*more
features
than
ever before*

ENGLISH DOGS:
First of a series of presentation prints

Houses of fantasy
and escape

HOUSE & GARDEN

JUNE 1961 THREE SHILLINGS

*Small gardens
in town & country*

*House & Garden
visits Italy*

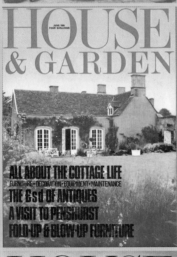

HOUSE & GARDEN

JUNE 1966 FOUR SHILLINGS

ALL ABOUT THE COTTAGE LIFE
FURNITURE • DECORATION • EQUIPMENT • MAINTENANCE

THE £s d OF ANTIQUES
A VISIT TO PENSHURST
FOLD-UP & BLOW-UP FURNITURE

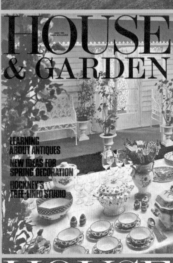

HOUSE & GARDEN

JUNE 1966 FOUR SHILLINGS

LEARNING
ABOUT ANTIQUES

NEW IDEAS FOR
SPRING DECORATION

HOCKNEY'S
TREE-LINED STUDIO

MARCH

House & Garden

Spring & Decoration

HOUSE & GARDEN

MARCH 1967 FOUR SHILLINGS

emphasis on
British design

ENGLISH DOGS: PRESENTATION PRINT

HOUSE & GARDEN

OCTOBER 1965 THREE SHILLINGS

*sketch-book
of
decoration
ideas*

All that's new from Scandinavia

HOUSE & GARDEN

OCTOBER 1965 THREE SHILLINGS

Scandinavian Round-up

HOUSE & GARDEN

OCTOBER 1965 THREE SHILLINGS

Town & country conversions • Beds & bedding • Town gardens

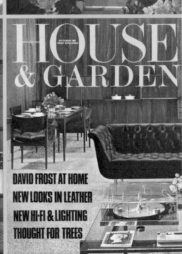

HOUSE & GARDEN

OCTOBER 1966 FOUR SHILLINGS

DAVID FROST AT HOME

NEW LOOKS IN LEATHER

NEW HI-FI & LIGHTING

THOUGHT FOR TREES

HOUSE & GARDEN

OCTOBER 1966 FOUR SHILLINGS

2
Stately
Homes
and
3
holiday
houses
IN COLOUR

Decoration
special

SOFAS
BEDSIDE TABLES
CURTAINS
STRETCH COVERS
LIGHTING
TV